History of the

1/1st Hants Royal Horse

Artillery

during the Great War, 1914-1919

Edited by Captain P. C. D. Mundy

The Naval & Military Press Ltd

published in association with

FIREPOWER
The Royal Artillery Museum
Woolwich

Published by
The Naval & Military Press Ltd
Unit 10 Ridgewood Industrial Park,
Uckfield, East Sussex,
TN22 5QE England
Tel: +44 (0) 1825 749494
Fax: +44 (0) 1825 765701
www.naval-military-press.com

in association with

FIREPOWER
The Royal Artillery Museum, Woolwich
www.firepower.org.uk

The Naval & Military
Press

MILITARY HISTORY AT YOUR
FINGERTIPS

... a unique and expanding series of reference works

Working in collaboration with the foremost
regiments and institutions, as well as acknowledged
experts in their field, N&MP have assembled a
formidable array of titles including technologically
advanced CD-ROMs and facsimile reprints of
impossible-to-find rarities.

STAFF-CAPTAIN THE PRINCE OF WALES, IN EGYPT
(MARCH-MAY, 1916).

List of Illustrations

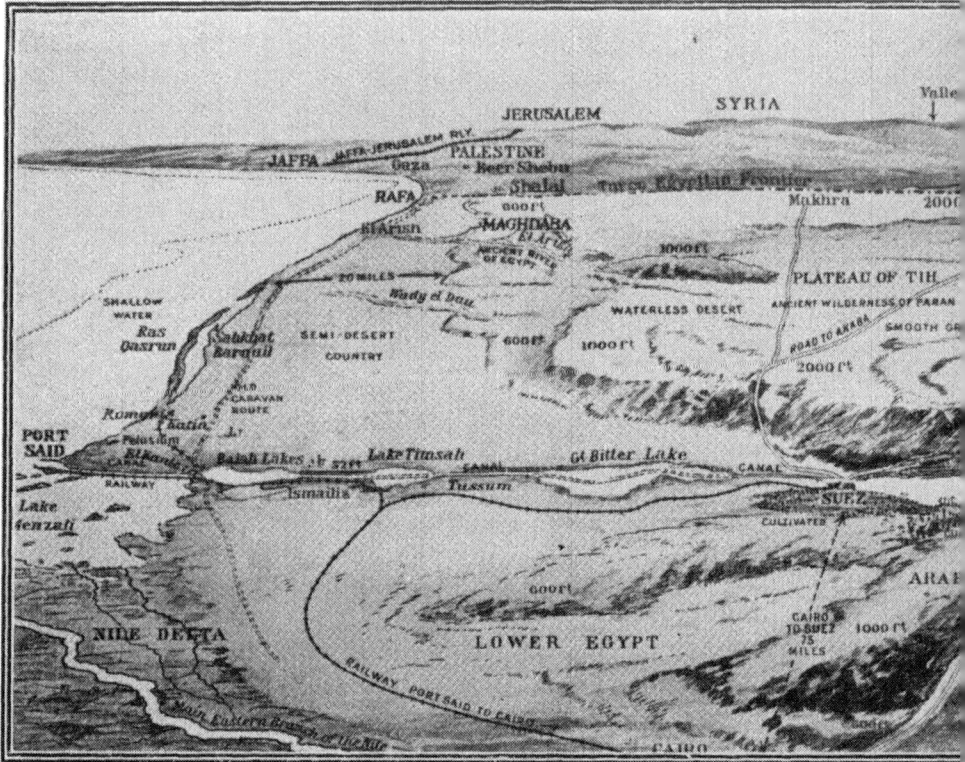

PANORAMIC VIEW OF SINAI PENINSULA.

(1)

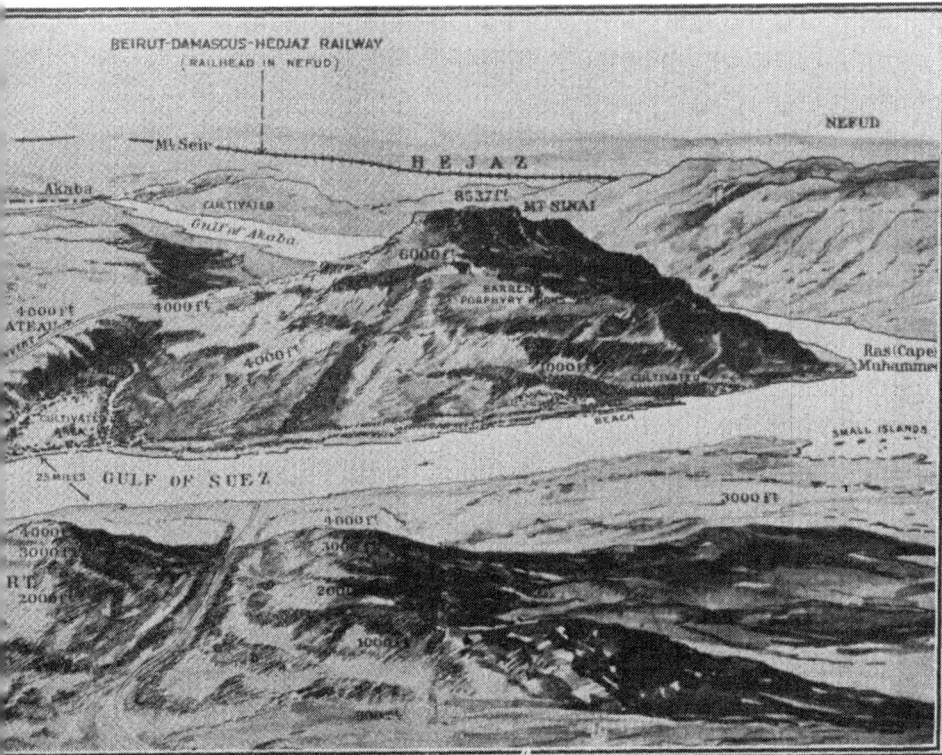

PANORAMIC VIEW OF SINAI PENINSULA.

(2)

Preface

A FEW WORDS are necessary regarding the intention of this volume, which records the war history of the 1/1st Hants Royal Horse Artillery.

Primarily, its object is to form a permanent memorial, not only of those who gave their lives for King and Country in the Great War, but also of those who were fortunate enough to pass safely through the conflict, and return once more—with unforgettable memories, and a wider vision—to their native county.

New generations are fast springing up to which the War will be little more than a tradition. It is well that these should be reminded of the splendid sacrifices and heroism of the older generation to which they owe an inestimable debt of gratitude.

Unfortunately, the record of the Battery for the opening period of the War is very scanty.

It was of necessity a time of action. There had been a sudden and dramatic change from the even tenor of civilian life (but recently resumed after the annual training in July, 1914) to the strenuous and unaccustomed conditions of active service.

The immensity of the issues at stake, and the volcanic upheaval which shook the foundations of every home, had obliterated minor interests.

The spirit of the time was not conducive to the leisurely occupation of keeping a diary.

Consequently, it has not been possible to chronicle fully or accurately the events of the period intervening between mobilisation and departure for active service.

Doubtless, individuals will recall many incidents—pleasant and otherwise—which will fill the gaps.

In making a selection from the material available for the purposes of this record, it has been the endeavour to omit nothing which bore upon the history of the campaigns in which the Battery took part.

An attempt has also been made to preserve picturesque details which revive memories of the lighter side of war, and of that spirit of comradeship which went so far to render bearable the inherent tedium and discomfort.

This cheerful endurance has always characterised the British soldier of all ranks and never was it so prominent or such a valuable asset as in the late war.

There are three main sources of information on which this volume is based.

First, the " War Diary," or Intelligence Summary (Army Form C. 2118) rendered to the War Office monthly by the Commanding Officer. Secondly, the full and unusually interesting diaries kept in the Battery; and, thirdly, notes from private diaries and extracts from letters.

Map references have been generally omitted. Without the inclusion of large-scale maps, which was impracticable, their value was insignificant.

Place names have proved a source of some difficulty, owing to the varied forms of spelling in different documents.

All the smaller illustrations have been contributed by photographers who actually served with this Battery*. The larger illustrations have been kindly lent by the Proprietor of *The Times History of the War*, a large and costly work in twenty volumes.

Special thanks are due to those who responded to a circular letter asking for information regarding certain periods of war service for which no data existed. Valuable services have also been rendered throughout the preparation of the work by Mr. A. C. Ashmead, acting as Secretary to the Committee.

THE EDITOR.

---

* Mr. S. R. Howard, Mr. W. H. Ponsford, Mr. R. F. Manning and Mr. A. C. Ashmead

History of the

1/1st Hants Royal Horse Artillery

during the Great War, 1914-1919

PONTOON BRIDGE OVER THE JORDAN AT GHORANIYEH.

History of the
1/1st Hants Royal Horse Artillery
during the Great War, 1914-1919

1914

AUGUST, 1914.

ON 4th August, mobilisation orders were received. Calling-up notices were immediately sent out, and in spite of many difficulties, and by means of the willing and zealous co-operation of all ranks, mobilisation was successfully accomplished at Southampton.

The following days were occupied in collecting horses and wagons, and in drawing ammunition. The horses were of a poor stamp, and the carts of a very miscellaneous description. The latter included a brake, known as " Queen of the Forest."

On 13th, the Right Sector left for Winchester—the War Station of the 1st South-Western Mounted Brigade—the Left Sector following a few days later.

A large number of the men were billeted in a brewery, and many more in a girls' boarding-school—it being holiday time. After about a fortnight a six days' march was undertaken to Forest Row, in Sussex. The route was via Cheriton, Petersfield, Midhurst, Billingshurst, and Crawley.

At Forest Row signatures were obtained of those willing to volunteer for foreign service. Needless to say, the greater part of the Battery volunteered.

The camp was formed under canvas in Kidbrooke Park.

SEPTEMBER, 1914.

On 10th September, Major M. B. F. Courage, Reserve of Officers, took over the command from Major Arderne.

Captain Gillson was transferred to Southampton to organise the 1/2nd Hants R.H.A. A move took place to Plaw Hatch.

The weather broke up, and there was much sickness among the horses.

OCTOBER, 1914.

The Battery and the Column were billeted in Plaw Hatch House and farm. Sheds were built for the horses, as they were suffering from exposure.

NOVEMBER, 1914.

Two journeys were made to London, to fire salutes at the funerals of Sir Charles Douglas and Earl Roberts.

DECEMBER, 1914.

Strenuous training was carried out, both as a Battery and with the Brigade.

1915

JANUARY, 1915.

The year opened with a Brigade day, carried out in a downpour of rain.

Little is recorded of the movements of the Battery during 1915.

Training was the rule, and many and various were the rumours of departure for foreign service.

The appearance of Major Courage in a trench-cap was productive of a fixed idea that the Battery was destined for the Western Front.   This persisted until the chauffeur of the Inspector of Remounts told the Sergeant-Major that he had seen a confidential document at the War Office which definitely consigned the Battery to the Dardanelles.

This rumour was confirmed by the arrival of four mules, and orders were shortly received for a move—to Eastbourne!

Here a Brigade Recruiting March was organised.   Much labour was expended on the "turn-out," and the result was said to be one recruit, who was subsequently turned down by the doctor.

In May, Major Courage and Major Joyce were transferred to the command of other batteries, and Captain Jeans was gazetted Temporary-Major, on taking over the command.

Many of the N.C.O.'s and men, who were skilled artificers were requisitioned for other duties outside the Battery, their places being filled by drafts from the second line at Southampton.

In July, the Battery and Column went into camp at Willingdon, near Eastbourne.

In August, five days' shooting was carried out at Okehampton.

In September, Brigade manoeuvres took place near Arundel, from 15th to 24th of the month.   The Battery supplied a Section to each force.

In October, the personnel consisted of 7 officers, 2 attached officers, 212 N.C.O.'s and men, and 13 attached N.C.O.'s and men.

In addition, 2 officers and 29 men from the second-line unit are shown as "attached for training."

Equipment was complete.   Transport, horses, and harness were in good condition, and the training and discipline was satisfactory.   The War Diary, dated 7th October, from Willingdon, shows that the Battery was quartered at Hailsham, and the Column at Polegate.

The War Diary, dated 7th November, states that " the Unit is now in winter quarters; Headquarters and Right Section at Woodside (between Polegate and Hailsham), Ammunition Column at Polegate, and Left Section at Hailsham."

On 26th November, there was an inspection by Major-General Brunker, Inspector of R.H.A. and R.F.A.

In December the strength, including attached N.C.O.'s and men, had increased to 263.

GAZA.

1916

JANUARY, 1916.

On 7th January, 1916, the Battery and Column proceeded to Lark Hill, on Salisbury Plain, to fire the final course prior to embarkation.

On 13th, the Battery joined the Brigade at Leicester, to form, with the Essex and the West Riding Batteries, the 1/5th Lowland Brigade Royal Horse Artillery.

The kindly and hospitable reception accorded by the people of Leicester is specially noted.

FEBRUARY, 1916.

On Thursday, 17th February, after a good send-off by the inhabitants, the Battery left Leicester to embark for service in Egypt. The morning was spent in loading stores at the railway station. The journey by rail was taken by night, the two trains departing respectively at 8 p.m. and 9.45 p.m., and arriving at Devonport at 9 a.m. and 10 a.m.

The Battery embarked on the H.M.T. "Manitou," a small and ugly-looking transport, which mounted a 4.7 gun. The accommodation available for horses and men was bad, owing to overcrowding, there being about a thousand of each on board. The ship sailed at 4 p.m., and was escorted by two destroyers for several miles. She commenced to roll as soon as she left the harbour, and maintained a list to starboard throughout the voyage. In the Bay of Biscay a fairly rough sea was encountered, and ninety-five per cent. of the officers and men suffered from seasickness. The Major, the Captain, the Sergeant-Major and two Sergeants were among the few who attended all parades.

On 21st, the coast of Portugal was sighted. On 23rd, at 4 a.m., Gibraltar was passed, and the calm waters of the Mediterranean formed a pleasant change. A magnificent panorama was afforded of the Sierra Nevada mountains.

The ship's run for the previous twenty-four hours was 284 miles, being about the average speed of the voyage—a rate of twelve-and-a-half knots.

On 24th, Oran was sighted, and the Algerian coast, with its snow-capped hills.

On 25th, when in the bay of Tunis, a distress signal was received by wireless. This subsequently proved to have been sent out by a destroyer which had been torpedoed by a submarine in the near vicinity of the ship's course. On the same day Malta was sighted, and British and French battleships were observed in the harbour, and patrol ships and destroyers outside. Large camps could be seen on the island.

On 27th and 28th, no land was in sight. On the latter day the Colonel gave a lecture on the best methods of avoiding sickness in a tropical climate.

At 3.30 p.m. on 29th, land was sighted about seventeen miles distant, and by 4 p.m. sand and palm trees could be distinguished.

On approaching closer, the harbour and town seemed to be gradually rising out of the sea, and by 4.45 p.m. there was a clear view of Alexandria.

The ship had to be in harbour by sunset, otherwise she would have to remain outside all night—possibly a prey to submarines.

Flags were hoisted—first the Blue Peter, then the Pilot flag. An Arab came on board, bringing the flag to be hoisted before entering the harbour. The ship was challenged at the entrance, and two heavy guns were trained on her. The harbour was full of British warships and troopships; also tramp steamers and hospital ships, whose green lights, combined with the yellow and red of the other ships, made a bright illumination in the evening.

The ship remained in port that night, and the conclusion of the voyage was celebrated by a concert.

The "Manitou" was generally considered a lucky ship. Three successive torpedoes had missed her previously, and she had been hit by a Turkish shell and set on fire. Throughout the voyage the weather had been fine. Rations were very indifferent, but there were no complaints. Deck quoits and other games, together with music, had passed the time pleasantly. The horses bore the journey well. Three only of the battery horses were lost, and these were on board the ship which brought over the Ammunition Column, which sailed a day before the "Manitou" and encountered the worst of the storm.

MARCH, 1916.

On 1st March, orders were received for the Brigade to proceed to Port Said. Some of the Battery had leave to go ashore. The heat was intense, and time did not suffice to see much of Alexandria, but the unfamiliar character of the streets and buildings, and the dress of the

EL KANTARA, ON THE SUEZ CANAL.

natives afforded considerable interest. That evening the ship sailed for Port Said.

Land was sighted at 9 a.m. on the 2nd, and the ship passed through the long breakwaters of the Suez Canal Harbour shortly afterwards.

British and French destroyers; British, French, Swedish and Dutch trading steamers seemed to almost fill the canal entrance.

The ship put in on the right-hand side, where another troopship was being loaded with stores, bound for France. The Battery was hailed with the cry of "Are you down-hearted?" The usual reply was given in concert. "Well, you very soon will be" was the comment from those who had experienced six months in Egypt—and they were not far wrong in their prophecy.

On disembarkation, a small advanced party of one officer—Lieutenant Kenning—and a few men proceeded to the camp allotted to the Battery, to investigate the facilities for watering, to draw forage, and to see that the camp generally was in order.

The baggage was off-loaded and placed on lighters. It was necessary for the men to have their blankets with them, also their kit-bags. These were taken in G.S. wagons to the camp, and a guard left with the rest of the baggage, as it was uncertain whether the Battery would remain at Port Said or not.

Guns were left at the quay under the guard.

The cleaning and coaling of the ships by natives afforded a good deal of interest. The speed at which they carried the coal in baskets up the narrow gangway, and threw it into the ship (not stopping if one of them fell down and was buried alive), was a remarkable sight.

On 4th, a small party proceeded to Kantara to take over a camp there. This camp had been vacated by a brigade of a division known as the "dirty worst." The condition of the camp fully justified the appellation. On Sunday, 5th, there was Church Parade at 9 a.m., at Port Said, and two short exercises for the horses. The party under Captain Pulteney at Kantara continued the arduous duty of cleaning the camp.

On 6th, the horses were exercised for the first time since disembarking, with the men mounted. Their condition was improving. To guard against sand colic, muzzles were obtained. During this week there were several bathing parades, and drill clothing and helmets were issued. Mosquitoes were much in evidence, and a sandstorm was experienced. News was prevalent that the Turks were about to sue for peace. On 11th the Brigade was inspected by Major-General Horne. The Battery found great difficulty in manœuvring in the sand. In the evenings football was played, and a visit was paid to the camp of the Mysore Lancers.

C

On 17th, a move was made to the camp at Kantara, and on the following day the first reinforcements, under Lieutenant Fleming, arrived from Alexandria. On 19th, letters from home arrived. Some of the men swam the canal; others fished—with little result.

On 20th, there was an inspection by Major-General Lawrence. One grey mullet was caught by a persevering fisherman of the Battery. Rations were improving: fresh meat, vegetables, marmalade or jam, rice, porridge and lime-juice were among the issues.

On 24th, the 52nd Division was inspected by General Murray. A detachment of the Mysore Lancers formed the escort, and the Prince of Wales was aide-de-camp to the General. The Prince rode a dark brown mare, and wore the insignia of the Grenadier Guards in his helmet.

On 27th, co-operation of artillery with air-craft was practised. The Divisional Band, consisting of brass band and pipers, played in the vicinity of the camp twice weekly. During the latter days of the month, gun drill was at 6.30 a.m., owing to the heat. The sand was so hot that it was impossible to walk on it with bare feet when bathing. Sandstorms were frequent. Scorpions and centipedes began to make an unwelcome appearance, in blankets and between sandbags.

APRIL, 1916.

On 3rd April, an Egyptian canteen was burned down by one of the brigades on the West bank, as a protest against the exorbitant prices charged for all foodstuffs. Two days later there was a clothing inspection at 8.30 a.m. to clear the Battery (and Brigade) of any suspicion of having participated in the theft of £150 in cash and certain goods from the Egyptian canteen, prior to its destruction.

On Sunday, 9th, the Battery Football Team played the Ammunition Column Football Team at 5 p.m.; the match resulted in a draw. On the following day the daily drill order for gun drill was held at 6.15 a.m. The Warwickshire Yeomanry joined the Worcesters at Katia. General Horne rode out beyond Katia with his staff and escort, and reported all clear for ten miles. An advance guard movement two days before had thrown the Turks back.

The first rumours of an offensive towards the Turkish base at El Arish, in which the Battery was to take part, were being circulated, and were received with great enthusiasm among the men.

On 11th, the 15th Army Corps, under command of General Horne, less the 52nd Division, left Egypt for service in France. Russian troops passed through the canal from Vladivostock on their way to Salonica.

THE DESERT RAILWAY.

A WELL AT EL ARISH.

Indian hours of parade were adopted. The routine was as follows:—
5 a.m., half feed; 5.45 a.m., tea; 6.15 a.m., gun drill; 6 a.m., exercise
horses; 7.30 a.m., water and half feed; 8 a.m., breakfast; 9 a.m., stables;
12.30 a.m., dinner; 2.30 p.m., water and feed; 4.30 p.m., water and feed;
5 p.m., sub. sec. gun drill; 6.15 p.m., feed.

On 13th, an unusually fierce sand storm was experienced. Tents were
blown down, and some of the men who were caught whilst bathing had
an unpleasant time. It was almost impossible to move outside the tents.
The food was full of sand, and innumerable flies took shelter within the
tents.

From 14th, shorts were allowed to be worn, and officers and men
appeared on all parades in shirt sleeves. Some catches of bass and mullet
were made.

On 17th, 40 Turks were captured in a raid on Jiffa-Jaffa.

On Easter Sunday, 23rd, at 3.30 p.m., an order was received for
one Battery of the Brigade to " stand by." The honour fell to the West
Riding Battery. It was rumoured that there had been a serious reverse
at Katia, and that artillery assistance was needed. Half-an-hour later
the whole brigade was ordered to harness up and proceed to the East
bank of the canal. The Brigade stood by all night. Early the next
morning eight aeroplanes passed over, en route for Katia. It was
subsequently learned that they had dropped bombs on parties of the enemy
grouped under the palm trees, and had effected considerable damage. The
absence of any further news of an action led to some depression, which
was instantly dispelled when the Battery itself was selected to proceed to
the scene of action, Hill 70, seven miles distant from Kantara. On
arrival there, on 24th, it was found that the Worcesters and the Warwicks
had sustained heavy casualties on the previous day. A day's work was
spent in improving the gun implacements, until they were practically ideal
from the point of view of protection, cover and comfort. Twelve Bedouin
prisoners were brought in. They were without uniform and dressed in the
ordinary Arab garb. The Battery—which was the first to leave the canal
and march into the desert of Sinai—now obtained the first impressions
of desert warfare. The disappointment was intense when the whole
Battery was ordered to return to Kantara, without having had the chance
of firing a single shot.

Bathing and fishing were two of the chief amusements. Diving-
boards were erected, and better sport was obtained from the East bank.
The best bait for bass, which ran up to 5lbs. in weight, was found to be
the long shellfish living in the clay, or a round shellfish, found only in one
spot along the canal, and discovered by Captain Elliott.

MAY, 1916.

On 2nd May, orders were received for the Battery to "stand by," and to sleep in their clothes. It was reported that the Turks had massed 10,000 troops at El Arish, and that they had three large guns and 30 field guns in Sinai, and that among the number were 1,000 Germans. This, it was rumoured, was the result of the evacuation of Kut.

On 3rd, a reconnaissance was made for position of guns for a firing practice, and three different platforms made for trial—concrete, wooden, and sand.

On 4th, the shooting practice was so successful that the Colonel paraded the Battery, and told them, in the presence of the officers of other batteries who were observing the shooting, that from beginning to end not a single mistake was detected. He praised both the speed and accuracy, and stated that the fire discipline was excellent. The wooden platforms were found to be the best, and finally adopted. The Battery thus gained the reputation for good shooting which was upheld throughout the period of service.

On 6th, the Battery was given a surprise "turn out," and accomplished the task in nine minutes. This constituted a record for the Brigade. The days were now becoming hotter and hotter, the maximum temperature being about 106 fahrenheit. Rumours were rife that the general plan was to draw the Turks beyond Katia, and that the Battery would move to Mahamdiya to assist in cutting them off from the flank.

On 8th, Major Jeans and Lieutenant Fleming proceeded to Mahamdiya to select gun positions; the railway was only completed as far as Pelusium, just short of Romani.

Sand tyres were tried on the gun wheels, and proved fairly successful. Also 12 horses (six abreast) were suggested and tried as a method of draught, but found to be unsatisfactory. Other methods were experimented with, but it was finally decided that 10 horses (two abreast), could not be improved upon.

In the afternoon of the 11th, the Battery was about to move off, when a sudden order was brought by a mounted orderly to the effect that the move was cancelled. The afternoon was spent, therefore, in bringing back the stores from the station, and in re-pitching the camp.

It appears that the move had been prepared against the advice of experts, who sent in reports that the water supply was not sufficient to meet the requirements of a Battery. It was also considered that a Battery in action five miles from a railway, and without adequate protection, would be in a most precarious position.

On 16th, the heat was almost unbearable. The men lay in their tents during the day without any clothing, trying to keep cool, but this was impossible with the temperature at 120 f. in the shade.

Even the natives declared that it was the hottest day they had ever experienced in that part of Egypt—the atmosphere being like that of a Turkish bath. As " battery on duty," breeches and putties had to be worn all day, which added to the discomfort.

On 19th, General Parker, B.G.R.A., introduced himself to the Battery, and gave an address, telling of some of his experiences with a mountain battery in India.

On 24th, a move, which had been ordered on the previous day, took place. Guns and stores were loaded on a special train, by means of a ramp of sleepers, the first one to be constructed on the railway, which played such an important part in the resulting campaign, in connecting the armies in Palestine with their base at Kantara. Officers and men found accommodation on gun or wagon limbers, or on corn sacks. The journey was along the new railway across the desert for 25 miles to Romani, or ultimate railhead.

An advanced party was sent to Mahamdiya to pitch the camp, and the Battery bivouacked at Romani for the night. Romani at this date consisted of palm trees and a few isolated tents, and there was no other artillery as far East—and very few troops—a great contrast to its appearance a few months later.

On the morning of 25th, the Battery moved off to Mahamdiya, four miles north. The journey was made over very loose sand, keeping in the valleys between the large sandhills, which looked like yellow snowdrifts.

The 4th Royal Scots provided an escort. In addition to six horses, infantrymen manned the drag-ropes (10 to each vehicle), but this method was found useless on the march, as the infantry could not keep pace with the horses, and consequently could not pull on the drag-ropes.

Immediately on arrival the guns came into action in gun positions which had been roughly prepared by a mountain battery.

A " mobile section " was formed out of "B" and "C" Sub-sections, their horses being in the best condition. All the horses returned to Romani under Captain Elliott and Lieutenant Kenning, keeping only four riding horses at Mahamdiya. The wagons and limbers were kept at Romani, 100 rounds of ammunition being dumped in each gun-pit. The drivers' camp was also at Romani.

The Right Section lines were laid out due East, covering Lake Bardawil (of gypsum—hard and dried up), whilst the Left Section was laid out South-east, with centre line on " Blair's Post."

Tracks were covered up, and red-coloured nets placed over the guns, to render them invisible from hostile aircraft.

Telephone communication was laid out, and the lines subsequently buried.

One officer and two detachments—sufficient to work the guns—were on duty from dawn till they were dismissed by the 156th Brigade H.Q., the officer sleeping at the observing station, and the men at the guns. The camp was first pitched about half-a-mile from the guns, and afterwards moved to within 500 yards.

The horses were brought to Mahamdiya every evening, and returned after dawn the next morning.

Water was brought up by camels, both for horses and men, from Romani, at the rate of 10 gallons per horse and one gallon per man. Rations were similarly obtained.

On 26th, it was reported that within five hours from any given time the place could be attacked by 5,000 Turks, mounted on trotting camels. The troops available at Mahamdiya amounted to nearly 4,000.

During the latter days of the month the gun positions were improved, a telephone-pit was dug for each Section, and observing station dug-outs commenced. Wells were dug at Romani to water the horses during the day.

On 31st, Major Jeans, Lieutenant Franklin and Lieutenant Fleming made a reconnaissance to choose a route for the Mobile Column, and suitable gun positions and observing stations. Hill 100 was found to be the best observing station, from which there was a wide field of view East and South-east as far as Katia.

The Australians carried out a reconnaissance in force almost as far as El Arish, killing 15 and capturing one prisoner.

JUNE, 1916.

On 1st June, a German aeroplane circled over the camp, and then flew over Romani, where it dropped six bombs, killing one officer and 10 men, and wounding 10 men. Thirty-six horses were killed, and a great many of the Australian horses broke loose. The Battery horses were watering at the time, under Lieutenant Fleming, who gave orders for the men to scatter with their horses. The Battery suffered no casualties. It was the first experience of hostile aircraft, and experience which increased in frequency and unpleasantness.

The 1/5th Lowland Brigade was now designated the 263rd Artillery Brigade, the 1/1st Hants R.H.A. being "A" Battery.

The decaville railway (2ft. 6in. gauge), from Port Said, had reached within a mile of Mahamdiya, and it was doubtful if that railway or the one from Romani would arrive first.

TURKISH PRISONERS TAKEN IN THE ROMANI BATTLE.

On 7th, reports were received that a hostile attack was contemplated, but a more reliable source placed the attack at the end of Ramadan (July), which is the Mohammedan equivalent for Lent.

On 7th and 9th, reconnaissances were carried out to discover a suitable track across the desert for guns, in the direction of Katia.

Only one practical route was found, and that presented serious obstacles, by reason of the heavy going and steep slopes. Some Egyptian jackals and foxes were seen, and a large turtle-shell was found by the old ruins of Mahamdiya, which must have been a considerable village. On this day news was received of the death of Lord Kitchener.

During the month the temperature of the sea increased daily, until it became unpleasantly hot. Three sharks were observed by bathers within forty yards of the shore. Immediately after recording this fact, the diary adds: "Three men were admitted to hospital." There appears, however, to be no connection between the two entries.

Much entertainment was afforded by the antics of hundreds of crabs, which lived in holes along the coast, and came out of the sea by hundreds. This particular species possessed eyes which resemble periscopes.

By 12th, both mentioned railways had reached Mahamdiya—the one from Port Said being the first to arrive there. It was reported that a reconnaissance in force to Bir-el-Abd, with two cavalry squadrons and one gun from the Somerset R.H.A., had resulted in two enemy casualties.

An aeroplane raid on Kantara took place—fifteen mules being killed. It was also believed that the enemy forces at El Arish consisted of 20,000 Turks, Germans and Austrians, but it was considered that an even larger force would find it impossible to face the strong defences of Mahamdiya.

On 15th, the Mobile Column paraded at 1.30 a.m. It consisted of two guns from the Right Section and one gun from the Left Section, with battery firing wagons, 10 horses to a team. The mobile portion of the whole Brigade was present.

Lieutenant Badcock was left in charge of details at the camp, and the remainder proceeded at 2 a.m. with the Brigade to El Rabah, seven miles across the desert eastward, over very heavy sand. This journey was accomplished without a single horse being galled. On arrival, there was no water available for the horses, as the Engineers who had been sent forward to dig wells, selected the low-lying, marshy ground in which to dig them, and in consequence found no water fit for horses to drink. Major Jeans secured some well lining and a pump from the R.E.'s, chose a spot which he considered a likely one, and had a well dug there. After a wait of seven hours the horses were at last able to have a good drink.

General Lawrence inspected the position intended for a bivouac for the Brigade that evening, and considering it unsuitable, ordered the whole Brigade to return at once.

At 7 p.m. the Battery set out for Romani. It was dark, and the route had not been reconnoitred, but the march was accomplished without a hitch by 10 p.m.

On the following day guns were dragged back to Mahamdiya, over very steep sandhills. They were brought into action the same evening, and the horses, being in very good condition before they started, showed little signs of fatigue. None refused his feed, and there were no galls, which reflected great credit on all, especially on the drivers.

On arrival it was learned that "B" and "C" Batteries had handed over their horses and received mules in exchange, but that "A" Battery was to retain its horses.

On 19th, 12 British aeroplanes bombed El Arish, doing considerable damage. Three, unfortunately, failed to return.

On 24th, Lieutenant Fleming returned from a secret mission, which had consisted in dragging in a British aeroplane which had fallen close to Ogratina.

On 27th, a German aeroplane passed over, and was pursued by a British aeroplane. On 28th, there was another fight in the air between a British and a German 'plane.

A machine-gun bullet pierced the oil tank of the British 'plane, forcing it to descend just as it was getting the upper hand. It landed by the shore, the 'plane being badly riddled.

JULY, 1916.

Of the early portion of this month there is little to record. Captain Pulteney returned to England on 6th. On 7th, a small percentage of the men were granted leave to Sidi Bish, whither the 156th Brigade proceeded for a rest; and the defences of Mahamdiya were taken over by the 157th Brigade.

The Kantara-Romani railway, which was being continued eastward, had now reached almost to El Rabah. The decaville railway from Port Said was now allowed to carry passengers, and was useful for mess stores.

On 9th, teams were sent out to bring in the engine of a British 'plane which had crashed close to Ogratina. Two days later a German aeroplane flew over. Four shots were fired at it by the Mountain Battery at Romani. On 11th, orders were received to proceed, shortly, to Kantara, giving up the positions to the Essex Battery. As so much work had been done, this was considered unreasonable, and every endeavour was made to avoid the move.

On 12th, Brigade H.Q. were moved from Kantara to Mahamdiya. An Expeditionary Force Canteen was opened for the first time.

Sharks were still observed near to the bathing places; and skate could be caught in the evening on a line cast from the shore.

On 18th, innoculation against para-typhoid commenced for all officers and men of the Battery.

On 20th, news came to hand that 8,000 Turks were advancing, and had reached Bir-el-Abd, 18 miles from Romani. The camp was struck and the Battery moved to Romani, all transport being carried out by camels —32 in number. The guns and wagons were pulled by 10 horses, and there was one spare pair for each team.

On arrival at Romani, orders were received for the guns to go into action on a dry marsh close to the railway on the South side, about half-a-mile west of railhead, with Hill 100 for their original line. The camp was pitched in the evening on the top edge of the sandhill, overlooking the marsh, on its southern side, with the wagon lines close up under the sandhill.

It was reported that eight to fifteen thousand Turks had reached Ogratina (twelve miles distant). Lieutenant Badcock and two signallers slept at the forward observing station on Hill 46, one-and-a-half miles N.E. by E. of the gun position, close behind Fort 8.

Troop trains were arriving all day, and the force at Romani was gradually doubled, reaching the number of 8,000 odd. The Australians were in touch with the Turks, and held them in check as they retired, and captured a few men. At night it was reported that the Australians were in touch with the Turkish patrols close to Katia (6 miles away). The Battery had orders to establish a mobile column ready to move out at any moment.

The other batteries at Romani were the West Riding, the Ayrshire R.H.A., and the Howitzer (263rd) Brigade. A patrol of infantry was told off to protect the Battery from surprise, from the southern and exposed flank.

The horses remained where they had been all the time—about a mile N.W. of Katib Ganit, the highest hill in the neighbourhood (228ft.) They were half-a-mile distant from the camp.

All guns were ready to open fire at any moment. There were 1,000 rounds in possession of the Battery. The camp was considered to be one of the best in the desert, as there were light breezes straight from the sea, even in the early morning. The only disadvantage was that a strong wind, such as blew nearly every afternoon at a later date, was apt to blow the sand from under the tent valences and smother the tent.

D

On 21st, two German aeroplanes flew over the guns, but it is unlikely that they could have seen them, as they were almost invisible in the brown marsh, especially when covered by the concealment nets.

The Colonel, who, in the absence of the Brigadier, was responsible for placing each brigade of artillery and allotting them their zones, was convinced that the main attack would come from the South. He gave orders, therefore, that the 1/1st Hants R.H.A. should move their guns so that they might be able to fire in an easterly and southerly direction.

On 22nd, a hostile aeroplane flew over, and a British 'plane, rising from the new aerodrome on the marsh N.E. of railhead, succeeded in driving it off, assisted by the fire of the Mountain Battery, which, however, did no damage. The British pilot was slightly injured.

All natives were now being sent back to Kantara from Romani, returning on the trains which brought troops. They had no liking for hostilities, and were not sorry to return.

The E.E.F. Canteen and the Y.M.C.A. at Romani were much appreciated.

On the night of 22nd, some natives attempted to break out of camp, in order to give information to the Turks. This attempt was frustrated. Nine Turkish prisoners were brought in, and news was to hand that 2,000 Turks, with seven guns, were digging in at Ogratina, that 8,000 Turks were at Mugeibra, eight miles due South, and that a very large number was concentrated at Bir-el-Abd, but that no attack was expected that night, or the next morning.

A section of 60-pounders arrived and took up a position 200 yards due north of the Battery, closer to the railway.

Major Jeans and Lieutenant Badcock went out on a mounted reconnaissance eastward as far as Hill 90, from which the enemy could be faintly seen through glasses.

On 24th, Lieutenant Franklin reported to the B.G.R.A., at Mahamdiya, to take a copy of the enemy position as located by aircraft, and the Australian patrols, and those of our infantry and artillery.

The enemy's position was more or less as reported, being dug in between Katia and Ogratina, with a large force at Mugeibra. Our own infantry was occupying a line from Mahamdiya to Romani, and were established in 10 or 11 small sand-bagged forts, the centre of the position being between Fort 7 and Fort 8, at railhead. The artillery was so placed that it could sweep the whole zone, and also the southern zone, where two forts were being hurriedly built.

On 25th, firing was heard in an easterly direction. It was reported to have been the Ayrshire Battery.

On 26th, Major Jeans and Lieutenant Fleming went out on a reconnaissance, in a southerly direction. The advanced guard of the Essex Battery arrived at Romani.

Major Jeans, who rode towards Katia with General Parker, the B.G.R.A., could see the Ayrshire Battery firing at the Turkish trenches.

On 27th, a message was dropped by an enemy aeroplane, asking that the hospitals might be more clearly defined by a large red cross, so that the aeroplanes could see them.

On 28th, it was reported that the Turks were advancing in force on Katia, and the Australians retiring, holding them well in check. The forward observing station had to be occupied during the day, as well as by night, by the orderly officer and two signallers. A new station had been constructed. A hole was dug out and a sandbag pit, with overhead cover and a slit for observation, was built. It was contrived so as to resemble a bush, and even at close range it could scarcely be distinguished from its surroundings.

Orders were received that evening for the Mobile Column to be ready to move off at 9.30 p.m., the Turks having advanced still further, and having taken Katia. All was ready for a move, but no final orders came through. Once more the Battery was disappointed, just when enthusiasm to go into action was at its height.

On 29th, little further information was received. It was rumoured that British aeroplanes could not obtain any information of Turkish movements in the southerly direction, and that some Staff officers were obliged to make a mounted reconnaissance in that direction.

Gun and rifle fire were heard in the afternoon, and it was stated that the Turks had two large guns in action in the neighbourhood of Katia. It was also reported that a patrol of Turks had pursued an Australian patrol to within a mile of the forts, and then retired.

Telephone wires were broken by camels, which frequently occurred, and linesmen from both ends went out.

On Sunday, 30th, the Leicestershire Battery, R.H.A., arrved in the night, and went into action on the southern side. Other troops also arrived.

On 31st, four enemy aeroplanes flew over and dropped 24 bombs. Two or three fell quite close to the horse lines, which were presumably their target, but did no damage. Further East, two horses were killed and four wounded. The men, who had not experienced being bombed, were exceptionally calm.

Another battery of howitzers arrived in the night, and more troops; also another section of 60-pounders, which went into action east of the battery position, with lines laid out in a southerly direction.

There were now 42 guns defending the position, and two monitors were off the coast at Mahamdiya. The total number of troops was approximately 15,000.

AUGUST, 1916.

On 1st August, a German aeroplane flew over the camp, both in the morning and in the afternoon.

One of the monitors fired 18 rounds at the Turks at Ogratina, with good results. Continuous firing was heard all day.

On 2nd, Major Jeans rode out on the southern flank on reconnaissance duty, to select a position in the event of a movement southward. The monitor kept up an intermittent fire on the Turkish trenches during the day. Enemy 'planes flew over, dropping several bombs, but without material result, though some fell very near. The enemy at this time had the ascendency over us in aircraft, rendered all the greater by the fact that there were no anti-aircraft guns on the spot. Some British 'planes flew over the enemy front lines in the afternoon. Enemy anti-aircraft shells could be seen bursting among them. The puffs appeared to be discharged in threes, proving that each shell had three bursts.

On 3rd, the sound of gunfire was heard at 6.30 a.m. in the direction of the Turkish lines, which were now much closer. Two German 'planes flew over Romani and dropped one bomb close to the F.O. station, probably intended for Fort 8. A de Havelin attacked, and a fight ensued, but the British 'plane was forced to descend very rapidly, owing to its machine-gun having jammed.

The monitors kept up an intermittent fire.

It was reported that the enemy were advancing their trenches from Katia towards Romani. Katia itself was occupied by the main force in the afternoon.

All were particularly on the alert now. A look of keenness and excitement was observable in every face. Gunners slept with the guns. A night attack was anticipated, but did not materialise.

On Friday, 4th, at 5 a.m., the enemy attack began with shell-fire on the infantry posts to the East and South, especially directed on Fort 6. Heavy rifle and machine-gun fire could be heard, and shrapnel could be seen bursting.

At 6 a.m., four enemy aeroplanes bombed the forts, camps, dumps and horse lines without doing any damage.

Howitzers, directed by aeroplanes, opened a very effective fire on Fort 6, and subsequently switched to Hill 59, on the left, and searched the camp of the Indian Camel Transport, on the immediate left of the gun position, killing 12 camels and dispersing a large number of the Egyptian Labour Corps, who disappeared over the hills.

At 6.55 a.m. the enemy infantry made an attack on Fort 6, and were repulsed. At 7 a.m., heavy howitzers commenced to search the ridge on which the camp was situated, adding 25 yards at each round.

Orders were given to take cover at the foot of the hill, which undoubtedly saved many casualties. The cook-house, a cook's-cart, and, worst of all, breakfasts, were destroyed by a direct hit. The Staff tent and its contents were riddled. The next round bracketed the telephonists —Bombardier Bannon and Gunner Wilkins—who, however, stuck to their job undisturbed. The Quartermaster's store tent had 84 holes in it.

At 7.15 a.m., the horses were taken off the lines and new lines prepared in a more covered position to the N.W. On being taken to water shortly afterwards, the parade came under shrapnel and rifle fire, but luckily no casualties were sustained.

In the meantime, a continuous bombardment of Fort 6, the dumps, camps, and observing positions was maintained throughout the day. Repeated infantry assaults were repulsed by artillery, rifle and machine-gun fire.

At 10.45 a.m., the Infantry Brigade reported enemy massing in Bir Abu Hamra, and three waves of infantry advanced in an attack on Fort 6. The Battery maintained a barrage between these two places.

At 11.25 a.m., the enemy commenced to entrench, but was checked by our fire.

Later, the enemy advanced in open order through Ghozlan, and was again stopped by our barrage, which was continued almost without interruption until 6 p.m. The West Riding and Essex Batteries were also firing on similar objectives during the day.

Second-Lieutenant Fleming, who had been in charge of the parade which at 7.30 a.m. came under shrapnel and machine-gun fire, had returned at 4 p.m. from a reconnaissance, and was on his way to replenish ammunition, when he was mortally wounded by a bomb from an aeroplane. He was taken to the 3rd Lowland Field Ambulance, where he died in a few hours, without having regained consciousness. This was the first casualty in the Battery, and the news was received with inexpressible grief.

At 6 p.m., orders were received to support the counter-attack of 156th Infantry Brigade against Wellington Ridge, which had been captured by the enemy. The ridge was searched and swept by salvoes. The attack was successful, and the infantry reported that the fire of the Hampshire Battery was just what was required.

The enemy continued to shell Fort 6 and the dumps throughout the night.

On the following day—5th August—intermittent enemy fire continued from an early hour in the morning. At 7 a.m., bombs were dropped by aeroplanes, but little damage was done. At 7.30 a.m., large numbers of prisoners were brought in, and a confinement camp erected to the right of the Battery's gun position. The final total number of prisoners amounted to 4,000. A battery of mountain howitzers, two sections of machine-guns, two field ambulance trains, and an enormous quantity of ammunition and stores were also captured.

The total enemy casualties (killed, wounded and missing) as officially estimated, amounted to about 9,000 out of a force of from 14,000 to 18,000.

At 9.45 a.m., orders were received to be ready to join the Mobile Column with 157th Infantry Brigade, under Brigadier-General Casson. At 10 a.m. the Battery marched to the rendezvous at Fort 8.

Orders were to clear Bir Abu Hamra of the enemy, and push on to Katia. The Battery accordingly took up a position behind Hod-el-Sofiya, whilst the infantry pushed on in a south-easterly direction.

At 4.15 p.m., the enemy heavily shelled Hod-el-Sofiya and Ghozlan. An hour or so later the Battery opened fire to support the 157th Brigade on the assault of Hill 74, firing salvoes as the infantry climbed the ridge.

The attack succeeded, and the enemy were driven off. The G.O.C. 157th Infantry Brigade expressed his satisfaction with the support received.

At 11 a.m. on Sunday, 6th, an advance was made to Katia, and a position was selected in the palm grove just north of the Great Tree, to cover a zone E. and S. The ground was smothered in offal and refuse left by the Turks, and the general condition aggravated by the stench of the horses and camels killed in the fighting on Easter Sunday. Large numbers of rifles, ammunition and stores had been abandoned by the enemy.

Throughout the evening the Turks continued to shell our positions with heavy field guns; and hostile aeroplanes bombed troops in the vicinity. Teams were sent out to bring in one of our aeroplanes which had been forced to descend. Never did bully beef and biscuits taste so good. Even the eternal marmalade was at a premium.

On 7th, there was again considerable activity in the air, and the palm groves were bombed by the enemy. News was received that the Turks had evacuated their positions at Ogratina, and had retired to Bir-el-Abd.

On 8th, new positions were prepared in the open, away from the intense filth of the palm grove, and the Battery remained in observation. At 10 a.m., there was a reconnaissance of officers and N.C.O.'s to Ogratina to examine the evacuated positions.

That evening the teams had a narrow escape when proceeding to fetch vehicles, the horse lines being bombed. Luckily there were no casualties.

On 10th, the Anzacs made an attack on the Turkish positions at

TUG-OF-WAR.

BATHING HORSES.

Bir-el-Abd.   The enemy, however, made a spirited counter-attack, and succeeded in driving off our troops, but sustained heavy casualties.

On 12th, orders were received to fix up a gun for anti-aircraft purposes. This was done with "D" Sub-Section gun.   A platform was made of brush-wood and sandbags on the top of a small mound, and the wheels and trail secured by sandbags.

The Turks were now retiring from Bir-el-Abd, whither the Anzacs and 5th Mounted Brigade had pressed them, harrassing them all the way. Before evacuating Bir-el-Abd they destroyed a large quauntity of stores and war material.

On the following day an opportunity occurred of testing the newly-contrived anti-aircraft gun.   Enemy 'planes flew over that evening at a much lower altitude.   Four rounds were fired, the first being remarkably close.

On 15th, the Division left Katia for Romani.   The Battery marched to a new position just to the left of the dump.   The 156th Infantry Brigade marched out from Romani to form an advanced protecting force to the railway, which had then reached Rabah.   The Battery came under the command of the G.O.C. 156th Infantry Brigade.

On 16th and 17th, enemy aeroplanes dropped bombs.   The heat was now intense, and one could not refrain from wondering why Providence had created flies!

Several cases of cholera had broken out, and consequently very rigorous restrictions and isolation were enforced.   The infection had no doubt arisen from contact with prisoners, and from the refuse previously referred to.   It was known that the disease was rife in Syria.

On 19th, the Battery was relieved by the Essex Battery, and returned to Romani, thankful to be back, and thoroughly appreciating cleanliness and comfort once more.

Inoculation against cholera was a minor trouble.   A week's rest followed, and it was not until 26th that the next move took place.   This was to Rabah, where the Battery took up a position 200 yards east of the palm grove.   The horse lines were in a small belt of palms, three-quarters-of-a-mile to the west.   Bivouacs were contrived out of palm leaves and blankets.   On 27th, two enemy 'planes came over and dropped hand-grenades among the Egyptian Labour Corps.   Two men were killed and several wounded.

On 28th, an anti-aircraft gun made its appearance, and on the following day enemy aeroplanes came over.   They received a real welcome from "Archibald."   Thirty-five rounds were fired, and "Fritz," taken by surprise, immediately hurried home.

SEPTEMBER, 1916.

The month of September opened with continued enemy attacks from the air. On 2nd, two aeroplanes bombed the dump and infantry bivouacs, killing three officers in the latter. On the following day further raids took place. One bomb fell within 15 yards of an officer of the Essex Battery, killing both his horses.

Strict instructions were issued as to the avoidance of the use of any Turkish utensils and material, with a view to the prevention of infection of cholera.

On 11th, the Battery quitted Rabah, and had an easy march to Romani.

On 16th, a well-deserved leave of 48 hours was granted to all ranks to the Rest Camp, Port Said. A party of one officer and 15 men proceeded thither. On 18th, this party returned. Food and accommodation were bad, owing to lack of organisation, and the result very unsatisfactory.

Several parades were held to practice co-operation with aircraft.

On 23rd, the Battery played the 91st Heavy Battery R.G.A. at football, and defeated them by three goals to one. On 24th there was a football match—Gunners v. Drivers. The former won. On 30th, there was a return match against the 91st Heavy Battery, who were again defeated.

On the whole, September was a quiet month, and the rest was thoroughly appreciated, after the recent strenuous conditions.

OCTOBER, 1916.

On 2nd October a six-a-side football tournament was started in the Battery. Each Sub-Section provided two teams; Brigade H.Q., Battery, Staff, Sergeants and Officers, one team each. The Colonel and the Doctor completed the Officers' team, which opened the tournament by vanquishing the Sergeants. The tournament was eventually won by a " C " Sub-section team.

On 3rd, Brigadier-General Parker, commanding 52nd Division of Artillery, presented to each Battery six small flags embroidered with its name, as a mark of his appreciation of the smart turn-out of the Brigade.

The horses were now looking very bad. This was due in part to the low quality of the forage, and in part to the excessively long walks to indifferent water. On an average, about 25 men were in hospital during the month.

On 16th, orders were received for the guns to be remottled red, blue and green.

On 21st, the Battery played a football match against the Essex Battery and won.

The railway had now reached Salmana, and the 52nd Division pushed on to new positions there. The rest camp at Sidi Bishr was to be closed at the end of the month.

On 25th, the Battery played and defeated "B" Battery H.A.C. by four goals to one, and on 28th scored a similar win against the 91st Heavy Battery.

NOVEMBER, 1916.

On 5th November, R.S.M. Faircloth received his commission, and R.S.M. Rishworth, West Riding Battery, took his place.

Second-Lieutenant R. Bazell was transferred from B.A.C. to the 1/1st Hants R.H.A.

On 13th, "B" Battery H.A.C. gave an excellent concert. A stage was fitted up at the end of the mess tent, and they produced their own stage furniture. The party consisted of a troupe of five pierrots, two being so well made-up as girls as to cause great *chagrin* to the audience when the delusion was discovered. Free beer added to the success of an enjoyable evening, which was attended by large numbers of the Brigade.

Firing practice in co-operation with aeroplanes was frequently carried out.

Owing to a number of cases of scarlet fever, and consequent isolation, the Battery was struck off Brigade duties on 22nd.

The railway had now reached Bir-el-Mazar, and the 42nd Division moved forward to take up positions there. On 27th, orders were received to be ready to move to a new camping site within the defences. An inner circle of forts had been prepared, the whole being enclosed in a barbed-wire ring.

On the following day the move took place, to a site about a quarter-of-a-mile to the S.E. of dump. The other units of the Brigade lent their sledges, and in consequence the move was accomplished with great ease.

During the month the following football matches were played:— The Battery v. R.A.M.C. (3rd Lowland F.A.), result—a draw; the Battery v. H.A.C., result—a win; the Battery v. the Essex Battery, result—a win.

DECEMBER, 1916.

On 4th December, the Commander-in-Chief, Sir A. Murray, visited Romani and inspected camps, etc.

A party was now detailed daily by the Battery on duty as look-out post on Katib Gannet.

On 9th, orders were received to be prepared to move to the southern sector of the Canal, at 24 hours' notice—an attack, presumably, being expected there as a counter to our offensive on El Arish. The railway

E

had now reached a point within fifteen miles of El Arish, and had temporarily stopped, it having been decided to attack the Turks from this base.

On 14th, information was received of the cancellation of this expected move.

On 20th, mounted troops entered El Arish without opposition, the Turks having evacuated their positions and retired to a new line, Raffa-Beersheeba. The Anzacs were followed closely by the 52nd Division.

A large number of evacuated trenches and gun positions were found facing the sea, proving that the enemy had expected an attack and landing from that quarter. The Navy co-operated with our forces—a landing-stage was erected, and large quantities of stores were put ashore.

The water supply all down the Wadi El Arish was excellent, and the ground hard and suitable for the quick and easy movement of troops.

Bursine was found growing around the huts and hovels composing the village.

On 21st, mounted troops and horse artillery pushed on to Maghdaba, to which post the Turks had retired on their line of retreat. The attack was commenced on the hostile positions at dawn with complete success, the very fine march of 25 miles from El Arish having been effected in four hours. The enemy was taken absolutely by surprise, with the result that seven guns and 1,330 prisoners fell into our hands.

Aerial reconnaissances reported that the Turkish bases of Hassana and Mekhyl had been evacuated, and that the whole of the Sinai Peninsula was again in our possession.

On 22nd, Captain Elliott and Q.-M.-S. Meaney went to Port Said to purchase beer and food for the canteen which it had been decided to open, the profits to be placed to the credit of the Battery fund. The experiment proved such a success that the stock was sold out the same evening.

Christmas Day opened with voluntary services at the Church Army Tent. Every effort was made to mark the occasion as far as was possible in the circumstances. Meals consisted of bacon and sausages for breakfast; roast beef, potatoes, cabbage, green peas and plum pudding for dinner. Fruit was also provided, and soup, custard and jelly for supper. A football match was played with the West Riding Battery in the afternoon, resulting in a draw.

Boxing Day was treated, as far as possible, as a holiday. A match was played between the Officers and Sergeants of the Brigade, which resulted in a draw. Heavy rain fell during the afternoon, and the weather became very cold, with a biting wind.

A message was received from his Majesty the King.

On 27th, the Brigade paraded at 9.45 a.m., and Colonel Robertson

R.A.V.C. DOSING A HORSE AT EL ARISH.

CAMP AT EL ARISH.

FARRIERS SHOEING A REFRACTORY MULE
AT EL ARISH.

made a speech, expressing his regret at the necessity of breaking up the West Riding Battery into two Sections, one of which was to join the 1/1st Hants R.H.A. Battery, and the other the Essex Battery. The Brigade was to be composed of two six-gun batteries of 18 pounders, whilst a battery of howitzers would be allotted at a future date. This re-arrangement was being effected throughout the Service. The Brigade-Commander took the opportunity to thank all ranks for their services and support in the past year, and wished them all good luck in 1917. Three cheers were given for the West Riding Battery.

The transfer of the Left Section of that Battery to the 1/1st Hants R.H.A. took place at 2 p.m.

On 28th, the new Sub-Sections were nominated "E" and "F", and formed the Left Section, whilst "C" and "D" Sub-Sections composed the Centre Section.

In the evening a concert was given by the choral talent of the Battery. A Bairnsfather sketch by Bombardier Bannon, and a short farce by Bombardier Taplin and Gunners Wiltshire, Davies, Grannel, Taylor and Gilbert proved most successful. The B.-S.-M., Sergeant-Wheeler Richardson, and Driver Loosemore, with several others, had greatly added to the effect by their untiring work in the erection of the stage at one end of the mess tent, and in the painting of the scenery.

This excellent concert was the last event of the year.

In addition to those football matches already noted, the Battery played the R.A.M.C. (3rd Lowland F.A.), and were defeated, and also the West Riding Battery, result—a draw.

Appendix No. 1.

No. 2 GROUP, 52nd DIVISIONAL ARTILLERY.
NARRATIVE 4th-8th AUGUST, 1916.

Additional to the Battery record, for a short period in the month of August, there is a narrative of No. 2 Group, 52nd Divisional Artillery, covering the period for the 4th to the 8th August, 1916.

The following is slightly abbreviated, and map references have been omitted:—

263rd BRIGADE R.H.A.

Romani, 4th August.

Enemy attack began at 05.00 with shell-fire on the infantry posts (especially on No. 6), artillery O.P.'s, F.O.O. stations and camel transport.

At 05.07 "C" Battery opened fire on machine-guns and snipers. Fire directed by F.O.O. in Post 6. After four rounds of gun-fire the telephone lines were cut, and a few minutes later Lieutenant Howkins was killed at the F.O.O. station by a shell which blew up the telephone dug-out. The operator escaped with a shock.

Second-Lieutenant Holberton replaced Lieutenant Howkins as F.O.O., and the lines were repaired under fire.

At 06.55 the enemy's infantry debouched from Bir Abu Hamra, and their advance was supported by Infantry Post Commanders at Post 6. "C" Battery shelled the advancing lines, which were checked and driven back to cover.

A second attempt, half-an-hour later, was directed against Post 6, and was driven back by "C" Battery.

The artillery telephone lines were cut at 08.00, and repaired three times at Post 6 under heavy shell and maxim gun-fire, the cuts being outside the parapet. Communication was maintained through the Infantry Post Commander.

The F.O.O. line being again in working order, a machine-gun was shelled with H.E.

At the same time "B" Battery was sweeping a spot where the enemy was observed massing behind a ridge. They dispersed, but re-assembled, and were again shelled out.

At 09.15 "C" Battery opened fire on Bir Abu Hambra. Searching and sweeping over a zone which had been previously registered. The fire was maintained at a slow rate for 20 minutes, and then switched on to low ground, where the enemy were collecting.

Successive lines of enemy infantry were seen crossing the ridges, and fire was lifted on to the crest, and continued at intervals as movement was observed.

At 10.20 an enemy Battery was observed by F.O.O. of "A" Battery, and the fire of "A" and "B" Batteries was concentrated on this target. No further movement was noticed.

At 10.45 the 158th Infantry Brigade reported enemy massing in Bir Abu Hamra, and three waves of infantry apparently advancing to attack Posts 5 and 6. "A" Battery was ordered to search and sweep between Bir Abu Hamra and Post 6.

The same order was given to "C" Battery. The group commander directed the alternative observation station to be used at Hill 125, instead of Post 6. Second-Lieutenant Holberton and the signallers then withdrew from Post 6, after six times renewing communications with the Battery under heavy fire.

Lieutenant Jackson took up F.O.O. duties at Hill 125, and gave very good reports throughout the day on the fire of the Group and on the enemy movements.

At 11.25 the enemy were checked debouching from Bir Abu Hamra, and they started entrenching.

Observation was difficult owing to the haze, and the ground was searched over by "A" Battery, whereupon entrenching ceased.

A little later B.G.R.A. informed the Group Commander that two enemy columns, 400 to 500 strong, were in Bir Abu Hamra. "C" Battery opened fire.

At midday Lieutenant Franklin reported as liaison officer to Colonel Walshe, C.R.A., Anzac Division, and arrangements were made for helio-communication and co-operation, if required. This was subsequently obtained in the attack on Wellington Ridge.

At 12.07 the enemy advanced in open order westwards through Ghozlan, and was met by gun-fire from "A" and "C" Batteries, and stopped. At the same time "B" Battery was ordered to search the palm trees in Hod-el-Sofiyla, from the point where the enemy had started entrenching to a position where they were collecting in dead ground. "C" Battery operated.

At 12.43 reports were received from the infantry that 2,000 enemy were advancing on Posts 4 and 5. "C" Battery was ordered to barrage the front of these posts, with Post 5 as the centre of the zone. This was continued for 20 minutes, and a second barrage was placed across Ghozlan by "A" Battery.

"B" Battery was ordered to search and sweep Hod-el-Sofiyla to drive back advancing infantry, and information sent to B.G.R.A. of the attack in force with the request that dead ground under Hill 59 might be enfiladed from Hill 115 by "A" Battery, 260th Brigade. This was carried out, and the enemy came under the concentrated fire of four batteries at this point.

At 13.50 fire was opened by the monitors off Mahamdiya, enfilading the front of the centre section, and observed by F.O.O. of "C" Battery as effective on the enemy infantry in front of Post 4.

During the afternoon "B" Battery fired on enemy skirmishers in Subket-el-Romani, and the F.O.O. caught some horsemen and led horses collecting, and afterwards shelled observers at that spot.

"C" Battery shelled enemy collecting in palm trees. Post Commander No. 6 Post reported enemy entrenching, about 100 strong, and "C" Battery shelled them with H.E. with good effect. The same party had been observed by F.O.O. of "B" Battery and fired on, the range being exact. "B" Battery continued on this target, together with "C" Battery, with 24 rounds H.E.

At 16.05 an enemy aeroplane dropped bombs, and one struck Lieutenant Fleming, of "A" Battery, who had come back from a reconnaissance, and was on his way to secure camels for Mobile Column work. He was rendered unconscious, and died a few hours later in hospital.

Further attempts by the enemy to mass troops, and to entrench were prevented by the fire of "B" and "C" Batteries.

At 18.10 orders were received to support with one battery the attack of the 156th Brigade to S.W. against Wellington Ridge.

Commencing at 18.45, "A" Battery reversed their guns and laid out lines of fire S.W.

In the meantime, "C" Battery maintained a slow rate of fire on the enemy entrenching, and "B" Battery did the same. Results were reported from Infantry Posts Commander as satisfactory, and the digging ceased.

At 18.45 the 156th Brigade attack began, supported by "A" Battery, searching and sweeping over the ridge. The attack was successful, and the 156th Infantry Brigade reported the fire of "A" Battery to have been just what was wanted.

At 19.15 "A" Battery was ordered to stand fast, ready to re-open fire on Wellington Ridge if required, and at 19.30 cease fire was ordered, preparations being made for night firing.

Casualties: 2 officers killed.

The following comments were made by Lieutenant-Colonel C. E. Robertson, Commanding No. 2 Group:—

Several instances of F.O.O.'s taking the initiative and dealing successfully with fleeting opportunities occurred, notably enemy infantry and camels observed advancing. The enemy were seen to scatter, and salvoes were fired over the area.

A railway cutting was shelled by F.O.O. of "A" Battery, who observed enemy massing under the banks. Enemy were also observed behind Bir Abu Hamra in large numbers, and shelled by F.O.O. of "C" Battery.

F.O.O.'s had instructions to take absolute control whenever they judged necessary, even to interrupting fire on a target engaged by B.C., and they took full advantage of this order. Their observation throughout the day was uniformly good, and communication of orders and co-operation with infantry by telephone and visual signalling had been practised on five days previously to the battle, under arrangements with H.Q., 158th Brigade, holding the Central Section.

Without this preliminary combined drill, in which F.O.O.'s, Post-Commanders, Infantry, Group H.Q., and Batteries were all experienced at the same time, it would not have been possible for the Group telephonists to have received and despatched the messages required for effective control, and in which seven operators were engaged with seven telephonists throughout the day. Practice in co-operation between artillery and infantry secured absolutely smooth working on the day, in spite of broken lines.

———◆———

No. 2 GROUP, 52nd DIVISIONAL ARTILLERY.
NARRATIVE 4th-8th AUGUST, 1916.
263rd BRIGADE, R.H.A.

Romani, 5th August.

03.00. Information received from B.G.R.A. as to operation orders for Anzac Division and Mounted Brigades. Post Commander No. 6 Post reported enemy thought to be bivouacking in Hod-el-Sofiyla. All quiet in front of Centre Section.

Subsequently F.O.O. reports from "A", "B", and "C" Batteries give visibility good and no signs of enemy.

At 06.52 F.O.O. "B" Battery reported that enemy were seen working and horsemen reconnoitring on Hill 74. This report was held to be doubtful, but proved correct, the enemy regaining a footing on the ridge till driven off by the 157th Infantry Brigade, supported by "A" Battery, about 6.30 p.m.

It was noteworthy that as the Anzac mounted troops were attacking Katia at 3 p.m. several hundred prisoners were brought in near "C" Battery F.O.O.'s station, and information received that large numbers were being collected by our mounted troops.

Second-Lieutenants Cruickshank and Davey joined "A" and "C" Batteries respectively to replace casualties of Lieutenant Fleming and Lieutenant Howkins.

At 09.45 "A" Battery was warned to be in readiness to join Mobile Column with 157th Brigade, under Brigadier-General Casson. The Battery marched to the rendezvous at Post 8 with teams of "C" Battery to allow for the "A" Battery teams to be fresh for work with the Column. "A" Battery took up a position of observation near post 7a, to cover the advance of 157th Brigade from Hill 100 to the S.E., clearing the ridges.

At 16.15 the enemy shelled Hod-el-Sofiyla and Chozlan heavily. The Anzac Division was observed attacking at Katia.

At 17.38 "A" Battery opened fire to support 156th Brigade in the assault of the ridge, and fired four salvoes as the infantry climbed the ridge. The attack succeeded, and the enemy were driven off. The G.O.C. 157th Brigade expressed his satisfaction at the support received from "A" Battery, the fire of which was observed to be very accurate.

Brigade Headquarters and "C" Battery received orders at midnight, 5th-6th August, to proceed on mobile column scale with 155th Brigade, the rendezvous being Post 5, at 3.30 a.m.

"C" Battery took up a position of observation to cover the advance to Katia.

"A" Battery was in a position of readiness near by, and "B" Battery remained at Romani.

At 11 a.m. the advance was made to Katia.

On 7th August, the Group, less "B" Battery, remained in observation at Katia. The enemy was active with aeroplane bombs.

On 8th August, new positions were taken up, and the Batteries remained in observation.

Reconnaissances of officers and N.C.O.'s to Ogratina to examine positions. "B" Battery at Romani.

Enemy aeroplanes bombed horse lines, but no casualties occurred.

1917

The record for the year 1917 is very unequal. The official diary exists for the months of January, September, October, November, and December. Information regarding the intervening period is an amalgamation of notes supplied from private diaries.

JANUARY, 1917.

The New Year opened with a high wind and a sandstorm. On the following day no gun-drill was possible, owing to torrential rains. Orders were received to fix draught bars for teams of twelve—four abreast—for the firing battery. It was found necessary to cover in the wheels of all vehicles with sheet tin, to prevent the sand getting over the edge of the sand tyres and forming a drag. This gave them somewhat the appearance of racing motor-cars—though, in the matter of progress, there was no resemblance.

The railway had now reached Bardawit, about ten miles from El Arish. On 3rd, the guns were taken out of action and parked at the north end of the camp. On 4th, a reconnaissance for all officers of the Brigade was ordered, for the purpose of selecting positions for a Field Day for all troops in Romani, but had to be cancelled owing to continuous rain.

On 6th, the Battery repeated the concert—previously given on 28th December—in the Y.M.C.A. Hut, which proved a great success.

On 9th, the Field Day for all troops took place; "A," "B," and "C" Sub-Sections used the four-abreast draught for the first time. In the evening the "Lena Ashwell Party" gave a performance at the Aerodrome, Mahamdiya; but, owing to the long day, the sixty-seven tickets allotted to the Battery were not used.

On 14th, the Battery mascot—the goat—having developed paralysis, had to be shot.

The remainder of the month passed uneventfully, until orders were received for a move up-country, and the camp was struck on 31st.

F

FEBRUARY, 1917.

On 1st February, the Battery quitted Romani at 9 a.m., leaving a small party to follow later. The march was via El Amara to El Rahbeh, where the night was spent. On the following day the Battery proceeded by Hod el Lisafah—where was noticed a huge cross erected to a dead German officer—and Hod Dawada, to Khirba. On 3rd, passing through Hod Daw Fitula, the Battery reached Bir el Abd, beyond which someone (with a perverted sense of humour) had reported that good roads would be experienced. As a matter of fact, the going was the worst encountered up to date. The route, continued via Salmaneh to Tilul, passing on the way a number of blockhouses.

On 5th, the march was resumed to El Mayar. The country was mostly marshy and low-lying, with slimy pools of brackish water; whilst the higher ground was dotted with miserable, stunted bushes, or brush, similar to that seen on some of the sandy stretches of Norfolk. A number of dead camels accentuated the depressing surroundings.

On the following day Maadan was reached by crossing the dry bed of Lake Badawil. Two flights of British aeroplanes—one of twenty-three and the other of eighteen—passed over towards the enemy lines.

At midday, on 8th, El Arish was reached. The town proved to be a dry, uninteresting place, about two miles from the sea. Near the coast is a small village called Um Jerrar, in the vicinity of which was the camp. Here the ground was cultivated, irrigation being accomplished by means of wells, from which small ditches carry the water to the allotments. Near by is the Wadi El Arish, dry in summer, but in flood within a few days of the Battery's arrival there.

On 15th, the site of the camp was moved to a fig plantation, near the Wadi.

On 20th, gun emplacements were in process of being dug.

The remainder of the month passed without any notable occurrences.

The Battery had managed to acquire a number of pets, including a Nanny-goat, with two young Billy-goats, a cat, and two tortoises. The antics of these animals caused much entertainment.

MARCH, 1917.

Very hot days, and equally cold nights, are chronicled for the month of March.

Training for mounted sports commenced on 17th, and on 24th the camp was moved to the site of the Nibi Jesir tomb. This was an ideal site —five minutes' walk from the sea, with the Divisional Band in the adjoining

HORSE LINES AT MAADAN *en route* FOR
EL ARISH.   FEB., 1917.

THE BATTERY PASSING THROUGH KHAN YUNIS, AT
FIRST ENTRY INTO PALESTINE.   APRIL, 1917.

"B" SUB GUN CAMOUFLAGED IN A CORNFIELD
AT SHEIKH NURAN. MAY, 1917.

GUN POSITION, SHEIKH NURAN.   MAY, 1917.

camp. This pleasant change after the solitude of the desert was much appreciated, as were facilities for bathing.

Rumours were current of a considerable engagement in front of Gaza, in which the 8th Battalion of the Hampshire Regiment had suffered severely. On 29th a continual stream of wounded was evidence of heavy fighting.

On 30th, four Taubes passed over, dropping bombs and killing and wounded many natives. On the same day six tanks, with their detachments, passed through, going up the line.

APRIL, 1917.

On 2nd April, a move was made from El Arish to El Burg, and thence by Shiek Zoweid to Rafa, on the borders of Egypt and Palestine. Much interest was taken in the stones marking the boundaries, and in the old frontier station. The fact that the sand had now given place to grass was also appreciated.

On 5th, the frontier into Palestine was crossed, and, after the desert, the Biblical impressions of the Holy Land seemed to be more than justified. A bivouac was formed in a cornfield, close to railhead, at Deir el Belah. The weather was very cold, and the next few days were taken up with gas-drill and general preparations for a move into the line.

On 14th, there was heavy shelling on the left flank, a great number of 5.9 shells falling on a C.C.S., with the result that, according to report, there were 41 killed and a considerable number wounded.

On 15th, a Taube dropped bombs, and caused the Church Parade to be dismissed.

There is little recorded in the diaries concerning the Second Battle of Gaza—16th to 28th April.

On 18th, heavy shelling on both sides is noted, and on 19th the gunners are stated to have had a heavy day, ammunition running short and having to be replenished from the Essex Battery. On 20th, the Battery retired two miles, and the infantry are recorded as "fighting all night."

On 22nd, the batteries on the left were firing throughout the day, and the weather was so cold that very little sleep was possible at night.

On 28th, a move was made to Shellal, and thence there was a thirteen miles' march to new positions in cornfields, in the vicinity of a great number of Turkish trenches. The Officers' Quarters were in a cactus hedge enclosure.

MAY, 1917.

The month opened with much enemy activity in the air.

On 5th, 6th and 7th, there were bombing raids on Belah.

Little information is available for this period until 22nd, when the Battery moved to a new position on the Wadi Ghuzee.

On 28th, three bombs were dropped near the guns.

JUNE, 1917.

The only recorded event is a heavy artillery bombardment on 11th, when the Battery stood to for two hours.

JULY, 1917.

On 5th July, the 18-pounder guns were handed over to a Welsh Battery, in exchange for 13-pounder guns.

On 6th, a move was made to the outskirts of Khan Junus for the purpose of a rest and to re-equip as Horse Artillery.

On the following day a camp was formed near the beach—a good bathing place for men and horses.

AUGUST, 1917.

On 18th, the Battery moved from Abasan to Tel el Farrah.

The only other event chronicled is an air duel between a British machine and a Taube on the last day of the month, on which date the Battery and Ammunition Column proceeded to Bir el Esani, in anti-aircraft formation, crossing the Wadi Ghuzzi at Goz Mabruk.

SEPTEMBER, 1917.

On 1st September the Brigade assembled in the Wadi, and proceeded to Rashed Bek; in which neighbourhood the Battery and main body of the Brigade went into a position in observation, whilst patrols maintained the line covering the reconnaissance of the 22nd Mounted Brigade to Azluz. A considerable amount of movement was noticed on the Beersheba—Khalusa road, but no target was presented.

During the month the Battery was constantly on the move, and took up several positions in readiness, but no notable events occurred.

On 18th, the Battery proceeded to the beach at Marakeb. On 28th, a gas demonstration was held in front of the camp.

OCTOBER, 1917.

On 12th October, orders were received that all R.H.A. Battery Ammunition Columns would be amalgamated, forming the three Sections of a Divisional Ammunition Column.

GUN POSITIONS AT SHELLAL, WADI GHUZZIE.
JUNE, 1917.

COOKS AND COOK-HOUSE AT SHELLAL.

BATTERY FIRING WAGON ON THE MOVE,
AT WADI GHUZZIE. JUNE, 1917.

COOK-HOUSE AT SHELLAL.   JULY, 1917.

GUN POSITION AT SHELLAL, IN THE WADI GHUZZIE,
JULY, 1917.

BIVOUACS AT SHELLAL, WADI GHUZZIE.   JULY, 1917.

BIVOUACS AT ABUSAN. AUG., 1917.

A HALT NEAR ABUSAN. SEPT., 1917.

"A" SUB DETACHMENT AT GAZA. 1917.

FORAGE CAMELS AT MARAKEB. OCT., 1917.

On 18th, this was carried out.

During the period spent on the beach at Marakeb time was, as far as possible, devoted to a rest for both men and horses. Sports of all kinds, including boxing, bathing, concerts, and other amusements were organised. At the same time training was carried out daily, consisting of Battery gun-drill, musketry, gas-drill, marching-drill, and staff rides. The general health was greatly improving, sick parade being reduced from fifty to sixteen.

The strength of the Battery was four officers and 162 other ranks.

On 25th, a move was made by Abusan el Kebir to Hiseia, and on the following day the Battery proceeded to Gozel Bazal, the headquarters of the 8th Mounted Brigade. On 26th, two Sections of the Battery were split up, and both were prepared to shoot at any moment during the night on receipt of a signal for help from the Yeomanry holding scattered trenches. On 27th, the Left Section received the S.O.S. signal, and opened fire with H.E. Heavy rifle and machine-gun fire was heard from the front-line trenches. No. 2 Gun, Left Section, was temporarily placed out of action with a shell jammed in the bore, but No. 1 Gun fired continuously. A message was received from a Squadron of Middlesex Yeomanry to the effect that it was nearly surrounded, and very heavily engaged by a large number of Turkish infantrymen. A Squadron of City of London Yeomanry was pushed up in support, and the Right Section opened fire with both guns. The 3rd County of London Yeomanry reported that they were unable to reach their objective, being very heavily engaged with shrapnel, machine-gun and rifle-fire. One group of Middlesex Yeomanry were driven in from El Buggar. Later, the Squadron in the trenches was reported completely cut off and surrounded. The Battery was then ordered to retire to new positions, but moved forward again an hour later and opened fire on enemy cavalry dismounted on a ridge, and continued from time to time to fire at various parties of cavalry. The 3rd Light Horse Brigade passed on the South, going East, in support.

During the afternoon the 53rd Division recaptured Point 630, and relieved the Squadron of Middlesex Yeomanry, which had held out to the last, having no ammunition left.

On 30th, orders were received to be prepared to move to any destination on the following day, within half-an-hour's notice.

On 31st, Beersheba was taken with 1,400 prisoners and nine guns.

NOVEMBER, 1917.

On the last day of October, the 20th Corps had attacked and captured

Beersheba, and the Brigade, which was expected to proceed there at any minute, remained in its bivouac in readiness to move.

No move actually took place until 4th November. On 5th, the Battery and the 8th Mounted Brigade marched to Beersheba, leaving the 18-pounder guns in the bivouac area in exchange for 13-pounder guns of the 19th Brigade R.H.A. On arrival, horses were watered in the Wadi, and the Battery proceeded to bivouacs in the area taken over from the 19th Brigade, R.H.A.

On 6th, the Battery remained in reserve in the neighbourhood of Khirbet el Muweilfe. The 53rd Division attacked north-east in the direction of Tel Khuweilfe, whilst the 74th Division pushed forward and stormed the work Kanwukah, and afterwards those of Sheria. The Yeomanry Mounted Division pushed forward between these Divisions. Two enemy 'planes dropped bombs in the vicinity of the Battery position, and three horses were hit.

On 7th, the Battery came under the orders of the G.O.C. 8th Mounted Brigade, and took up a position covering the front held by the Brigade.

Fire was opened on an enemy battery, and on a troop of cavalry.

Information was received that the Turks were withdrawing, and on 8th the Battery came into position, covering the advance northwards towards Bir Abu Khuff of the 8th Mounted Brigade; and subsequently advanced with that Brigade to a certain position in order to cover the watering of the horses, which already had been twenty-four hours without water. Unfortunately, the well could not be located, and a further advance had to be made without water.

Fire was opened by an enemy 10-pounder, from the high land on the right flank of the advancing Brigade, and orders were given by the G.O.C. 8th Mounted Brigade to engage this Battery and, if possible, silence it.

Lieutenant Bazell located the Battery and took control of fire, with excellent results. The enemy was forced to change his position. Fire was also opened on ridges where it was thought that enemy guns were concealed.

In the meantime, the 8th Mounted Brigade had advanced, and had pushed forward a dismounted attack from the hills. The Battery received orders to advance in support of this attack. This was effected, but owing to the exhaustion of the horses, it was found necessary to withdraw from the attack and retire to Sheria. The Battery opened an effective fire on the ridges overlooking those held by our troops, and the withdrawal of the Brigade was completed without loss.

Sheria was in an extremely foul condition, being strewn with dead; whilst animals, stores, and ammunition were littered about everywhere as the enemy had left them in his retreat.

The Battery shortly moved to Huj, which place had been charged with great gallantry by the 5th Mounted Brigade on the previous day.

On 10th, the Battery, with the 8th Mounted Brigade, moved to Jemmamel, and subsequently to Tel el Nejili, and to a point two miles east of El Mejdel.

On 12th, the Battery, with the 8th Mounted Brigade, moved off northwards along the road to Esdud, where the Brigade took over the line held by the Anzac Division. This area consisted of sand dunes.

On the same day the 52nd Division attacked and pushed forward to the ridges north-east of the villages of Burka and Yasur.

On 13th, the Battery moved to a position just south-west of Khirbet Sukerir; whilst the Yeomanry pushed forward to Tel el Kharrube. Fire was opened on trenches on the south side of Yebua village, from which place the Brigade was held up by the rifle and machine-gun fire. A brisk bombardment of the trenches occasioned the withdrawal of the Turks, whereupon the Brigade galloped into Yebua with drawn swords, taking the village and pushing beyond the bridge. The Battery advanced to a position among fig trees and cactus hedges a quarter of a mile west of the village. Fire was opened on the village of El Kubeibe, and on the ridges towards Zernuka, and was maintained on groups of the enemy during the whole afternoon.

The City of London Yeomanry pushed forward to attack Kubeibe, but were held up by heavy machine-gun fire; at the same time two Squadrons of the Middlesex Yeonmanry, after considerable fighting, occupied Zerneka.

During the day the 52nd Division had occupied a line just south of El Mansura, whilst the 6th Mounted Brigade galloped into El Mughar, taking 1,000 prisoners and two guns, and suffering about 150 casualties.

The 22nd Mounted Brigade took Akir on 14th, and on the same day Nannal was captured by the 8th Mounted Brigade.

The Battery shelled the ridges, which were strongly held by the enemy, and was itself heavily shelled by 75's, but luckily escaped casualties. Fire was also opend on Tel Bukkish.

On 15th, the 6th and 22nd Mounted Brigades were ordered to attack Abu Shushe, where the 8th Mounted Brigade was to maintain the line which it had been holding during the night. It was found that the enemy had evacuated his position and retired northwards through Ramleh and Ludd. The attack on Abu Shushe having been successful, the 8th Mounted Brigade advanced into Rahleh. The Battery took up a position covering the village of Jimzu.

On the following day the Anzac Division entered Jaffa, the 8th Mounted Brigade pushed forward through Ludd, and the Battery took up a position in the olive groves half-a-mile to the north of the village of Ludd. Observation was obtained from the top of a high tree, and fire was opened on enemy cavalry.

On 18th, information was received that the enemy were evacuating Jerusalem. Owing to the ruggedness of the route and its remoteness from the base, it was considered highly improbable that supplies could arrive. So orders were now issued authorising troops to live on the country, and to allow no opportunity to pass of watering horses and filling water-bottles.

The Battery left Ramleh on the morning of the 18th, and proceeded to Annabi, where it was found that all wheeled transport had to be left, owing to the road being impassable.

The Battery pushed on through Berfilya to El Burg, where it arrived after a most trying and difficult march, over great limestone rocks and day to Beit-ur-el-Zalita. The remaining two Batteries of the R.H.A. Brigade were turned back with the Divisional wheeled transport, the tracks being considered impassable. The Hants Battery, however, by dint of infinite care, trouble, and energy by all ranks, were enabled to proceed with their Brigade, which was acting as advance guard. The going was now so bad that the Yeomanry were unable to ride, and were forced to lead their horses along the dry bed of a mountain torrent, with banks rising from 100ft. to 250ft. on either side, until help up by snipers and machine-guns. The G.O.C. 8th Mounted Brigade decided that it was impossible for the guns to proceed further, and on 20th the G.O.C. Yeomanry Division issued orders to the same effect, and the Battery returned to Ramleh.

On 24th, Major Jeans returned from leave in the United Kingdom, and again took over command of the Battery.

On 26th, seven aeroplanes bombed troops in the Ramleh area, and the Hampshire Section of Yeomanry Divisional Ammunition Column suffered heavily in casualties to horses.

DECEMBER, 1917.

The official War Diary for December 1917 shows that the line was being held by very thinly-scattered posts. Companies of 163rd Brigade being very weak after past operations, and consequently the infantry being somewhat nervous of the situation, it was more than ever necessary for the artillery, sparse though it then was, to give every support.

On the 1st, a target was engaged in the Wadi Natief. Lieutenant Thomson left to report as liaison officer to 233rd Infantry Brigade, on the right of 163rd Infantry Brigade; whilst at the same time two batteries of 18-pounders and one 4.5 howitzer battery were brought up in support of this front.

The whole of the artillery in this sector was placed under two groups.

The infantry being thus reinforced, it was possible to close up the chain of posts, the whole being moved left towards the N.W. The rearrangement of the line necessitated a change of F.O.O.'s, and the Battery now established one of these with the Battalion headquarters of the 1/4th Wiltshire Regiment. A Company of the 1/4th Hampshire Regiment had become involved, being unable to extricate itself from a hill to which it had pushed forward, owing to machine-guns and snipers on the flank. The Battery opened fire on the ridges held by the enemy, with the result that the Company was enabled to withdraw without further loss.

On 2nd, Major Jeans, being in the F.O.O, observed and engaged an enemy O.P.

On 3rd, the Battery was relieved by "B" Battery, 37th R.F.A., and proceeded to Jimzu, where it bivouacked for the night.

On the following day, a guide, furnished by 263rd Brigade R.F.A., arrived to take the Battery to its new position. The line of march was along the track through Jimzu, Berfilya. A line of fire was laid out through Shilta. The Left Section registered upon a point where enemy machine-guns had been situated. Night lines were registered, the Right Section in Shilta and the Left Section in a Wadi, and communication was established with 263rd Brigade Headquarters at El Burg, at which spot were regimental headquarters of the Warwickshire Yeomanry, who were then holding the line covered by the Battery.

Owing to the lack of water, the majority of the horses had to be sent back, only forty-eight being able to remain. The Battery was thus split up. There was the party at the guns, consisting of four officers and 72 other ranks, with 48 horses, whose rations and forage were sent up daily from Latron by arrangement of the Australian Division; whilst the other party, consisting of one officer, 67 other ranks, and 114 horses, returned to Jimzu.

On 5th, the front line was advanced to Shilta-Suffa, the enemy having evacuated these points and retired to the depth of a mile. On the same day fire was opened, at the request of the O.C. the Gloucestershire Yeomanry, upon a party of Turks. Night lines were registered upon Deir el Kuddis.

On 6th and 7th, fire was opened upon machine-guns. On the latter day rain commenced, and the conditions for men and horses were very bad.

On 8th, fire was opened on a redoubt at Deir el Kuddis, and machine-guns were also shelled. Owing to the heavy rain which had fallen during the last twenty-four hours, the difficulties of transport were great. No rations were drawn. In pouring rain, orders were received to prepare to

G

relieve "B" Battery, 263rd Brigade R.F.A., at a position 1,000 yards north-east of El Burg. Before the position had been reached, however, the relief was countermanded, and the Right Section had to bivouac in the darkness where it stood, on heavy mud, in pouring rain.

On the following day, the Left Section engaged Turkish patrols at Sheik er Rafaty. A very short issue of rations was received. Four teams of six were temporarily attached to the Battery for the purpose of drawing ammunition wagons of the Hampshire Section of the B.A.C., which had been placed out of action by bombs whilst at Ramleh, ten days previously.

On 10th, orders were received to move forward and relieve 68th Battery R.F.A., and instructions were issued that the expenditure of ammunition was not to exceed twenty rounds per gun per day, save under extreme necessity. Targets were engaged in the neighbourhood of Deir el Kuddis, these chiefly consisting of small parties of snipers and machine-guns.

On 11th, 12th, 13th, and 14th, similar targets were continuously engaged. Owing to sickness, the Battery was 14 men under strength, and horses were showing signs of recent hard work and lack of forage. The Australian Division was still upon mobile forage and rations, consequently the Battery fared ill in comparison with other units, which drew full forage and rations daily. The Battery was also thirteen horses short, without winter clothing, and seriously in need of equipment and stores of all kinds.

On 14th, the first pay was issued since 20th October, money being obtained from the Desert Corps Field Cashier.

On 15th, the Veterinary Officer of the South African Field Artillery was called in to inspect the horses. He reported that he considered there were 20 horses which should at once be cast, and that unless some improvement was made in the near future, with regard to forage, facilities for watering, and provision of rugs, nosebags, and other stores, a considerable number of the remainder of the horses would prove unsuitable for the work.

On 16th and 17th, small parties and observation posts were frequently shelled, and a prisoner of war stated that the shell-fire had been very accurate and disturbing to the enemy.

From 18th to 26th, machine-gun emplacements, enemy ration parties, working parties, and similar movements were constantly shelled. On 24th, Lieutenant R. Bazell rejoined the Battery, having been unfit for duty owing to septic feet, contracted whilst detached from the Battery at Beit Foka, where he was awarded the Military Cross for gallantry.

Information had been received that the enemy intended to attack our positions in front of that portion of the line held by 53rd Division on the extreme right; and it was proposed to forestall his efforts by a counter-attack of the remainder of the 20th Corps to the left. The Australian Division was

THE BATTERY IN THE JUDEAN HILLS. NOV., 1917.

THE 1/1ST HANTS R.H.A. CAMP AT MEJDEL. JAN., 1918.

ordered to conform to these intentions, and to demonstrate on its front, thus preventing the reinforcement of the enemy by a lateral movement of troops from West to East.

It had been the intention for some time to shorten the line by pushing forward the 20th Corps on the right, in order that the front, instead of running obliquely from the advanced position of the 21st Corps on the sea, should run perpendicularly to the coast.

The Australian Division, to which the Battery was attached, being sandwiched between both Corps, pushed forward whilst the Battery maintained its fire on enemy O.P.'s, machine-gun emplacements, and sangars. The line of ridges running through Kuddis was finally reached. The attack of the Divisions on the right having been extremely successful, the Australian Division retired to its previous line, as originally intended.

The Battery was then relieved, and withdrew to Latron.

On 28th, the Battery trekked via Junction Station to Mesmiyeh, and on the following day it left for Mejdel, where it rejoined the Yeomanry Mounted Division, coming under orders of the O.C. 20th Brigade, R.H.A.

The guns, which had been severely shaken and damaged by the bad roads, and by the impossibility of keeping them in condition, owing to lack of stores, were left at the ordnance workshops at Junction Station. A thorough refit of all necessaries and equipment was commenced, and large numbers of horses had to be cast.

On the last day of the month and year orders were received to prepare to move to Deir el Belah.

———◆———

The following extracts from a private diary are published as supplementary to the official record for a short period of the latter part of the year 1917:—

25th October, 1917. Camping on the seashore. Orders to move; so packed up and trekked to Shellal.

26th October, 1917. Left Shellal, and were on a " stunt " towards Beersheba, and went into action at 5 p.m.

27th October, 1917. Stood to at 3.15 a.m., and opened fire at 3.45 a.m. In action all day, firing very heavily until relieved by another battery.

28th October, 1917. Nothing doing. Quiet days.

30th October, 1917. Went across the Wadi and camped.

31st October, 1917. Beersheba captured, with 1,400 prisoners and nine guns, etc.

1st November, 1917. Gaza heavily shelled all day.

2nd November, 1917. Two lines of trenches and 300 prisoners captured near Gaza; also two new pumping arrangements and storage for 10,000 gallons of water.

3rd November, 1917. The 6th Mounted Brigade captured two field guns and a few prisoners.

4th November, 1917. We left Hiseia for Gozel Bazal, where we stopped the night.

5th November, 1917. Left Gozel Bazal and passed through Beersheba. Changed our 18-pounder guns with the Essex Battery for 13-pounder guns.

6th November, 1917. Turkish positions attacked nine miles north of Beersheba. We had some horses killed by a bomb.

7th November, 1917. Gaza captured. Big haul of booty and prisoners. Sheria captured; 4,000 prisoners and 1,000,000 rounds of gun ammunition.

8th November, 1917. Left Sheria and went East towards Gaza front, where the Warwick Yeomanry charged and captured eight large guns.

9th November, 1917. Turks retreating along the whole front. Busily engaged in following them up.

10th November, 1917. Went across towards Beersheba front, and kept on after the Turks all day.

11th November, 1917. Turks retreated during the night. Following them up from the Eastern front, across up to the coast to Jesuid.

12th November, 1917. Jesuid captured, after fighting all day.

13th November, 1917. In action all day at Yebnah, 1,000 prisoners taken.

14th November, 1917. Kadis taken. Turks retreating northwards.

15th November, 1917. Captured Ramleh. The church bells rang—the first time for three years.

16th November, 1917. Ludd taken, with 390 prisoners and two machine-guns.

17th November, 1917. Went back to Ramleh for a day's rest.

18th November, 1917. Pursuing the Turks again. The Battery proceeded over the Babylonian Hills towards Jerusalem.

19th November, 1917. Proceeding over more rough country. Guns and wagons upset.

20th November, 1917. Discovered impossible to cross over the rocky hills with the guns, as there were no passes; so we returned to Ramleh.

21st November, 1917. Resting at Ramleh.

22nd November, 1917. Still resting.

23rd November, 1917. Fighting still going on in the hills.

24th November, 1917. Mounted troops hard pressed in the hills.

25th November, 1917. Leicester Battery returned to the hills.

26th November, 1917. Berkshire Battery returned to the hills.

27th November, 1917. Raid by enemy 'planes. Bombs dropped near Ramleh, doing great damage among horses. Night raid; no damage done.

28th November, 1917. Battery moved into position, three miles east of Ludd.

29th November, 1917. Taubes paid us a visit, machine-gunning the troops from low altitudes.

30th November, 1917. Battery moved into position, 2,000 yards further east of Ludd.

1st December, 1917. Battery fired on Turkish working-parties and patrols. Good results.

2nd December, 1917. Taubes raided Ramleh during the night, dropping bombs and machine-gunning the troops in the vicinity.

3rd December, 1917. Turks heavily shelled our positions.

4th December, 1917. Battery returned to the hills. Only 70 men and 48 horses allowed to remain there, the remainder returning to Jimzu.

5th December, 1917. Battery in action. Ammunition sent up from Jimzu.

6th December, 1917. Battery still in action. Raining all day.

7th December, 1917. Ditto.

8th December, 1917. Still in action.

9th December, 1917. Bethlehem captured. Battery advanced 2,000 yards in very bad weather.

10th December, 1917. Jerusalem captured. Battery still in action.

11th to 15th December, 1917. Still in action, but nothing important happened.

16th December, 1917. Four Taubes bombed Jimzu.

17th to 26th December, 1917. Battery remained in action. Very bad weather; raining nearly all the time Lieutenant Bazell awarded the Military Cross. He brought us up some things for Christmas; but it rained all day. Caplin awarded the Military Medal.

27th December, 1917. Relieved from action by the Notts R.H.A., and returned to Latron, where we camped for the night.

28th December, 1917. Left Latron and proceeded to Railway Junction, where the guns were put into the A.O.C.

1918

JANUARY, 1918.

The close of the year 1917 found the Battery at El Mejdel, but on 1st January, 1918, orders were received for a move to Deir el Belah. Lieutenant Bazell, with four teams, proceeded to Junction Station to fetch guns from Ordnance workshops, and on 2nd January the Battery left El Mejdel at 7.30 a.m. and marched to Gaza, arriving about 3 p.m. A small dismounted party proceeded by train to Belah with a number of heavy stores and tents. The night was spent in bivouac at Gaza. The following morning the Battery moved off at 8 a.m., and marched to Deir el Belah, arriving about 2 p.m. Here the dismounted party joined the unit, and the camp was pitched.

On 5th January, Lieut. Bazell, with four guns and teams, arrived from Junction Station.

Normal training, and the usual routine continued throughout the month, without any special events to chronicle.

The strength of the unit at the close of the month was six officers and 160 other ranks.

FEBRUARY, 1918.

On 7th February, B.G.R.A. Desert Corps, Brigadier-General King,* inspected the horses in the lines, and expressed himself very pleased with their appearance.

On 12th, the G.O.C. Yeomanry Mounted Division conducted a tactical ride for Unit Commanders, and a week later the 8th Mounted Brigade Field Exercises took place at Khan Yunis.

On 20th, orders were received that, owing to the Mounted Brigade being required for salvage work on the old trench line south of Gaza, the Yeomanry Mounted Division would move to that place. Accordingly, on 22nd, the Battery moved to a camping site south-east of Ali Muntar.

On 27th, Brigadier-General King inspected the Battery in drill order. An advance and a retirement were carried out, and the General expressed

---

*Colonel (Temp.-Brigadier-General) A. B'A. King, C.B., D.S.O., r.p. (R. of O.).

BATTERY COOKS AT GAZA. FEB., 1918.

HORSE LINES AT ENAB. APRIL, 1918.

his satisfaction with the turn-out, the appearance of the horses, and the manœuvring of the Battery.

During the month there were two or three drill orders each week, and every opportunity was afforded for outdoor exercise. Considerable interest was shown in the Divisional Football Cup. The health of the Battery was very good, there being on an average not more than three or four other ranks reporting sick daily, out of a total strength of 171.

MARCH, 1918.

On 17th March, orders were received for a move to Sukerier, and on 12th the Battery proceeded to Mejdel, where it bivouacked for the night. On the following day a camp was formed 500 yards south-west of Khirbet Sukerier. On 13th, the G.O.C. Yeomanry Mounted Division, Major-General G. de S. Barrow*, inspected the horses in the lines. On 16th, Lieutenant Findlay proceeded to the Imperial School of Instruction at Zeitoun for a gunnery course, and Lieutenant G. V. H. Mansell was temporarily attached during his absence.

Lieutenant R. Bazell proceeded to 20th Brigade Headquarters, on 17th, as Acting Adjutant, during the absence of Captain Buxton. On 23rd, there was a Battery Staff Ride at Ras Deiran, under B.G.R.A. Desert Mounted Corps, and again on 30th, at Ayun Kara. On the latter date orders were issued for the Yeomanry Mounted Division to move to Deir el Belah, and on the following day it was announced that the Yeomanry Mounted Division would be broken up, eight regiments being dismounted and formed into Machine Gun Battalions.

APRIL, 1918.

On 1st April, the Battery set out for Deir el Belah, staying the night at Deir Seneid en route. On 15th, there was an inspection by Brigadier-General King. On 23rd, Major T. K. Jeans, M.C., was admitted to hospital. Captain R. D. Badcock, M.C., taking over command.

On 24th, orders were received that the 20th Brigade, R.H.A., would march to Talat el Dumm, remaining the night at Gaza.

On 25th, the Battery marched to Mejdel, where it bivouacked for the night, and the following day the march was continued to Junction Station. The next night was spent at Enab, and on 28th Talat el Dumm was reached.

On 29th, a reconnaissance for Battery Commanders, under Lieutenant-Colonel Eugster, commanding 20th Brigade R.H.A., was carried out with Colonel Onslow, of the 7th A.L.H. Regiment, for the purpose of selecting positions for the attack on Kabr-Said and Medju Dieh early on the morning of the 30th.

---

*Major-General Sir G. de S. Barrow, K.C.M.G., C.B., *p.s.c.*

On that day the Battery left its bivouac area and proceeded to Maraadet Hajla, where a pontoon bridge had been thrown across the River Jordan.

This was crossed by unharnessing horses and leading them over singly, vehicles being man-handled. The Battery then took up a position, and came into action in the open, though screened by scrub and small bushes. Lines were laid out on Kabr Mujaaid.

The Patiala Infantry Battalions attacked and took the positions. Lieutenant Thomson was sent out as F.O.O. Fire was opened on a ridge which was lined by enemy infantry and machine guns, and which dominated the position which our infantry had seized. The enemy opened fire on the Battery position with mountain guns. The position of the infantry was unsatisfactory, being dominated and outflanked on all sides on the high ground and mountains which bordered the absolutely flat and open plain on which the battery position was situated. With a few short intervals, fire was kept up throughout the day, and the enemy responded. Although able to distinguish the flashes, owing to camouflage he was unable to see the guns themselves.

During the rest of the morning and afternoon the enemy maintained a constant intermittent bombardment. Shells actually burst between and all around the guns, splintering the wheels, but failing to cause any casualties. Later in the day the enemy fire abated, and the Battery withdrew to El Ghoranyie, the retirement being covered by the Patiala Infantry.

MAY 1918.

Having spent the night of 30th April in bivouac, orders were received on the following day that the Battery would support an attack of the New Zealand Mounted Brigade. A reconnaissance was carried out by Battery Commanders, and the C.O., 20th Brigade R.H.A., but previous instructions were cancelled and the 20th Brigade was placed under the C.O., 302nd Brigade, R.F.A.

The Battery was brought into action again in the open, among the scrub, and opened fire on Der Basi, in support of the 179th Infantry Brigade. Lieutenant Findlay was sent forward as F.O.O., to report to the C.O., 2/17th London Regiment. Fire was opened on various bodies of Turks and machine guns.

Subsequently orders were received to be prepared to support the attack of the 179th Infantry Brigade, and to demonstrate during the assault of the 181st Brigade, in positions on the left front.

These orders were cancelled, and two demonstrations of ten minutes' duration were carried out.

On 2nd, Lieutenant T. E. Holberton relieved Lieutenant V. A. C. Findlay

"C" SUB WAGON LINE IN THE JORDAN VALLEY.
MAY, 1918.

BATHING IN THE JORDAN. MAY, 1918.

as F.O.O.   Targets were engaged immediately on Makkar Derbasi, and occasionally in the wadis and hills further to the east.

The Turks, who had evidently ranged with a camel gun in the morning, now opened fire with a 10.9 Continental howitzer, several shots falling very close to the guns.   A bombardment of enemy positions was carried out in conjunction with all batteries of 302 F.A.B. Group.   The Wellington Mounted Rifles opened communication with this Battery on the right.

On 3rd, there was a ten minutes' bombardment of the plateau in Makkar Derbasi.

Lieutenant Mansell relieved Lieutenant Holberton as F.O.O.   Targets were again engaged.   The O.C. F.A.B. Group visited the battery position, and stated that the G.O.C. 179th Infantry Brigade and the O.C. 22nd Battalion the London Regiment had asked him to express their satisfaction with the work of the Battery, and the manner in which the F.O.O.'s had carried out their duties.

At midday the Turks opened fire with 10.9 and 77mm. guns on the battery position, it being very easy for them to see the flashes of the guns.

Lieutenant J. H. R. Thomson was wounded by a splinter of a 10.9 shell, and was admitted to hospital.   During the rest of the day, on each occasion on which the Battery opened fire, the enemy replied, chiefly on No. 1 gun.

On the morning of 4th a bombardment of enemy positions, of one hour's duration, was maintained.   Fire was commenced on Makkar Derbasi, at the rate of one round per gun per minute for ten minutes, and subsequently increased to the rate of two rounds per gun per minute.

This bombardment drew fire from the enemy; one other rank in No. 1 gun was slightly wounded and two horses in the wagon lines were hit. During the morning, and up till 1 p.m., various targets were engaged. That night the Battery withdrew, marching back to Ghoraniyie, where it went into bivouac on the east bank of the Jordan.

On 5th, the Turks shelled the outer defences.   Orders were received that the Battery would cease to be under command of O.C. 302nd F.A.B. Group, and would get into communication with O.C. 20th Brigade R.H.A., with a view of obtaining further orders.

A reconnaissance was carried out, under O.C., 20th Brigade R.H.A., for battery positions in defence of the bridgehead.   Positions were selected, with observation from the hills immediately in rear.   The position was in the midst of thick undergrowth and scrub, and the guns were effectively covered from view from the air.

The order was to " stand to " daily at 4 a.m. until receipt of "all clear." At 4 p.m. targets were registered in front of the wire, and at various points to the south.   Major T. K. Jeans, M.C., returned from hospital, and took

H

over command of 20th Brigade R.H.A. during Colonel O. L. Eugster's absence, as Group Commander, Captain R. D. Badcock, M.C., continuing in command of the Battery.

B.G.R.A. 60th Division expressed his thanks for the work of the Battery during its attachment to the 302nd F.A.B. Group.

On 7th, an enemy aeroplane dropped three bombs in the vicinity of the wagon lines, but without causing any damage.

A reconnaissance was made for a position further to the west. Shortly afterwards orders were received for a move, and an O.P. was selected 150 yards to the right of the gun position, which was under cover and hidden from view from the air.

It was arranged that the F.O.O. should be found by each Battery on successive days, on which days that Battery would be in observation, and that the O.P. would be manned by an officer, whilst visual communication was established with F.O.O. and a look-out kept all night for S.O.S. flares.

B.G.R.A. Desert Corps inspected the positions on the following day. The heat in these hollows was intense. There was practically no breeze, and the relaxing nature of the atmosphere made it necessary to do as little work as possible between 9 a.m. and 4 p.m., in order to maintain the health of the troops.

On 12th, the 1st Mounted Division relieved the Anzac Mounted Division in the Ghoraniyie sector. Major-General G. de S. Barrow inspected the battery position and considered it very suitable.

On 13th, the 20th Infantry Brigade relieved the 181st Infantry Brigade in Ghoraniyie bridgehead defences.

On 16th, orders were received to reconnoitre for a position to cover a possible enemy attempt to cross the River Jordan at Makhad et Hajla and at El Henu.

On 20th and 21st, reconnaissances were carried out in accordance with instructions from 20th Brigade R.H.A. for the purpose of selecting an alternative gun position, and another route out on to the top of the plain, to the west, without proceeding along the main road.

On 22nd, a reconnaissance was carried out to Makhad et Hajla and El Henu. The gun position there was finally decided upon, and ranges, angles of sight, and bearings taken.

On 25th, the Turks pushed up a gun and shelled the west bank of the river and the watering-place at the ford. A reconnaissance was made to Wadi Nueiame for a suitable place for horses to water out of observation and if possible out of range.

On 27th, on account of continued shell-fire, the wagon lines were moved out of range, to the west.

A large number of men were evacuated to hospital during the month. The climatic conditions of the Jordan Valley proved very trying to. all ranks. The greater number of the men, though not actually sick, were often not fit for duty. A large number of men were taken to be trade tested, which increased the burden on the remainder.

The strength of the Battery on the last day of the month was four officers, 141 other ranks, and 169 horses.

JUNE, 1918.

On 1st June, the Battery took its turn on observation duty.

On 3rd, 250,000 rounds of S.A.A. were dumped at the battery position, to be issued by the unit as required to troops at bridgehead.

In order to relieve the personnel of R.H.A. Batteries in the Jordan Valley, a camp was formed at Enab, under arrangements of Desert Mounted Corps. The establishment of Batteries was to be temporarily reduced. This Battery being considerably under establishment, was not able to sent the full quota. The party consisted of 25 other ranks and 50 horses. It left camp for Talat el Dumm on the 4th.

On 12th, Lieutenant Holberton, having been granted three weeks' furlough to the United Kingdom, left forthwith.

On 15th, minor operations by the 29th Lancers were to be carried out on the east bank of the Jordan. One section, under Lieutenant G. V. H. Mansell, proceeded to a position, where it came into action in a position covering the retirement of the cavalry, should they need support. The operations were successful, but the section did not open fire, and returned to the battery position.

On 16th, one Section, under Lieutenant Mansell, took up a position in observation, crossing the ford at El Henu.

On 17th, the 6th and 8th Mounted Brigades carried out a sweep of the country on the east bank of the Jordan. Lieutenant Drake, Leicester R.H.A., acted as F.O.O. to the Section of the 1/1st Hants R.H.A. Our Cavalry withdrew without difficulty, and no artillery support was required.

On 18th, information was received from a prisoner of war that it was the intention of the enemy to attack. All possible precautions were accordingly taken.

On 22nd, the first party from Enab returned, and on the following day the second party proceeded thither. This consisted of 20 men and 45 horses, 20 of the latter having been left behind by the first party.

On 25th, there was unusual enemy artillery activity.

On 28th, orders were received for a move, under cover of darkness, to Makadet Hajla. At 7.30 p.m., teams left the battery position and proceeded to Ain Hajla. An attack was considered imminent, and the rôle of the Battery was to delay a crossing of the fords by the enemy.

Communication was established by telephone with H.Q. Dorset Yeomanry and H.Q. 6th Mounted Brigade, and arrangements were made to send out an F.O.O. immediately to the threatened point as soon as that spot was definitely established.

Owing to the great length of front on which it was possible for the enemy to attempt to bridge the River Jordan, it was considered better to retain the F.O.O. with the Battery, than to send him to a place that might not be threatened.

On 29th, the C.R.A., Right Sector, Desert Mounted Corps, visited the Battery. He considered the position unsatisfactory, and a reconnaissance was therefore made for a better one. This was found very difficult to secure, owing to the nature of the ground—all hollows running west to east to the River Jordan, and none north to south—and owing to the difficulty of having both fords under effective range.

On this day the Battery was relieved, and became Mobile Corps Reserve, bivouacking at Wadi Kelt.

The party from Enab returned.

The rate of sickness during the month showed a marked increase.

JULY, 1918.

On 1st July, pools were found, cleaned and deepened, and a trough and pump put up in the Wadi Kelt. A very good supply of excellent water was thus obtained for the horses, and their condition improved wonderfully in consequence.

A reconnaissance was carried out of the Hajlah and Henu defences by the G.O.C. 6th Mounted Brigade (Brigadier-General Godwin).

Major T. K. Jeans, M.C., temporarily detached to command 20th Brigade R.H.A., was admitted to hospital, Captain R. D. Badcock being in command.

On 6th, Lieutenant G. V. H. Mansell proceeded on special leave to Egypt. On 7th, Major T. K. Jeans returned from hospital to command the 20th Brigade, R.H.A. On 8th, Lieut.-Colonel Frost, commanding 303rd F.A.B., visited the Battery and discussed the scheme of defence for Hajlah and Henu areas. Sergeant Schofield, A., was taken round the posts and shown the scheme of defence, with a view to forward observing. Owing to there being only two officers in the Battery, it was necessary for sergeants to do the duties of the former.

On 9th, a reconnaissance was made towards the Aujah Sector, and

THE RIVER JORDAN.

THE BATTERY ENTERING THE HILLS ON THE WAY TO
THE JORDAN VALLEY.

possible battery positions selected, in order to be able to bring fire to bear between the Aujah and Ghoraniyeh bridgeheads.

On 10th, P.H. helmets were issued to all ranks—40 per cent. of these were found to be defective.

During the night of 13th and 14th, a considerable amount of heavy gun-fire could be heard on the Aujah and Nablus fronts; as day broke considerable amount of artillery activity developed in the Ghoraniyie Sector, and to the south thereof. On the latter date orders were received for the battery to be prepared to move at a moment's notice.

It was reported that the Turks had advanced under cover of darkness, and were now holding a line on the edge of the broken ground, with their right flank thrown back along the line of the Wadi er Rameh. It was not proposed to bring the guns into action until nightfall unless a serious attack should develop but horses remained harnessed up in readiness for a sudden move.

The plan was to endeavour to turn the enemy's left flank, and charge him from the south with two squadrons of Johdpur Lancers. Simultaneously a mounted frontal attack was to be made by the Mysore Lancers, and similar action on the enemy's right flank by the Sherwood Rangers. It was considered whether one section should be brought forward into the actual river valley, but it was decided better to keep the enemy in ignorance of the presence of the guns should his attack materialise on the night of the 14th instant.

The attack in question was carried out with complete success, the enemy being driven back in great disorder. Their losses were 90 killed and 76 taken prisoner.

On the following day patrols failed to get in touch with the enemy. On 22nd, news was received that the Battery would shortly move out of the Jordan Valley. This move commenced on 23rd, and after bivouacking a night at Talat el Dumm the Battery, together with the remainder of the Brigade, reached Enab. On 25th, the March was continued to Latron, and on 27th a further move was made, via Naane, to Deiran, where a standing camp was made, tents being erected. The horses had stood their long trek well, and were in good hard condition.

Considerable reinforcements were received to replace casualties due to sickness. These reinforcements consisted largely of men who had not even an elementary knowledge of gunnery (one only having been in an R.H.A. Battery), and scarcely any were able to ride. This necessitated training of the most elementary kind.

The number of sick admitted to hospital during the month was one officer and 26 other ranks.

AUGUST, 1918.

The horses, which had stood the journey from the Jordan Valley very well, now appeared to be going back in condition, owing to the presence of colic.

The camp at Deiran being upon sandy ground, application was made to move to a fresh site off the sand.

On 7th, the 43rd Divisional Cavalry illustrated the advance of cavalry through a trench system which had just been assaulted by infantry.

On 8th, the site of the camp was moved on to black soil, and the condition of the horses showed immediate improvement.

On 25th, the 20th Brigade R.H.A. marched to Mejdel, via Wadi Surar.

Latterly, the state of sickness had decreased, but an unusually large proportion of the men were suffering from boils, debility and minor ailments, and consequently unfit for duty, though remaining with the unit.

SEPTEMBER, 1918.

During the first week of September normal routine and training continued, without any special occurrences to chronicle.

On 10th, orders were received from 20th Brigade R.H.A. that Battery Commanders, with one gun and a full detachment and three signallers and horse-holders, would proceed to Muelebis on the following day. All moves were to be made by night, and the utmost secrecy was to be observed. The remainder of the Battery was to be prepared to move on the night of the 12th.

All surplus stores were at once collected and moved to the station for transfer by rail to Desert Mounted Corps Dump, at Ludd. Sights and buffers were tested, and every preparation was made for active operations, the Battery being now up to full establishment in horses.

On 12th, the Battery left Mejdel for Junction Station, one gun having proceeded there on the previous day. On 13th, the Battery remained in bivouac for the day, and the next day marched to Ludd, where it went into concealed bivouac areas in the olive trees. The single gun, which was 24 hours in advance, marched to Muelebis and bivouacked in concealment among gum trees.

The very strictest care and precautions were enforced, no fires being lighted by day, no bivouacs erected, and no animals removed from the lines except within the wood where troughs had been erected. Every precaution was taken to avoid leakage of information as to concentration. On 15th, the remaining three guns arrived from Ludd.

On 14th, orders were received that the 1/1st Hants R.H.A. would be responsible for the defence of the line on their immediate front.   Accordingly, full detachments and signallers were moved to the gun position, where great care was taken to ensure that men should keep under cover of the nets.   No rations or forage were provided, and the arrangements for these were very poor.

The barrage table having been prepared during the previous days, full preparations were made for the 19th, which was the date selected for an advance.

One hundred and fifty rounds had been allowed for registration and 220 rounds per gun were dumped at each gun-pit.   These were carefully sorted into heaps and lots, each heap having the exact number of rounds required for each lift of the barrage.

The firing battery wagons and first line wagons were concealed in orange groves, east of Sarona.

On 18th, a reconnaissance was made for the rendezvous of the 4th Cavalry Division after the completion of the barrage, which was practised two or three times to ensure that all ranks were thoroughly acquainted with their work.

On 19th, the barrage was carried out with complete success, the infantry obtaining all their objectives, and immediately after its cessation preparations were made to advance.   Gun teams and lead horses arrived, and the Battery limbered up and proceeded to the rendezvous.   Owing to a slight error, the cavalry had already passed, and a long trot was necessary before the Battery regained its position behind the leading squadron of the second Regiment (the Middlesex Yeomanry), the 11th Cavalry Brigade being in advance.

The Turkish wire and trenches which had previously been demolished and filled in, were passed, and the Brigade proceeded at a steady pace, the going being heavy, in a northerly direction.   After a halt, an advance was made to where a small rearguard of Turks was still holding certain trenches. The Battery came into action, but did not open fire, as the enemy at once retreated, and it was not desirable to disclose the presence of artillery.

The advance was continued, after a halt of three hours for food and water, to Kakon, where a further halt of an hour and three-quarters occurred.   The next halt was at Lejjun, which was reached at breakfast-time on the morning of 20th.   The Brigade subsequently advanced to Beisan, via El Fule, where the Battery bivouacked for the night, having covered 85 miles in 37 hours, without the loss of an animal.

On the following day a reconnaissance was made with a view to the defence of Beisan, should the enemy strike north in force.   It was, however, very difficult to decide on a position, there being no commanding point of observation. Finally, a position was selected 300 yards west of the village of Beisan, on the south side of the road.

Orders were received that evening to occupy this position in support of the 10th Cavalry Brigade. No instructions were received from this Brigade, but communication was established by telephone with the headquarters of the Dorsetshire Yeomanry, who were holding some advanced posts 4,000 yards south of the village. An F.O.O. was sent out to one of these posts. The O.C. Dorsetshire Yeomanry reported several thousands of the enemy approaching the posts, and requested the Battery to open fire. This was done, and the area in front of our posts, on both sides of the road, was searched and swept with good moral effect upon the enemy, as large numbers soon afterwards gave themselves up, and the attack came to an end.

On 23rd, the 11th Cavalry Brigade went south to round up prisoners on the Jordan, leaving the Battery in position at Beisan. An hour and a half later the F.O.O. reported that the Brigade was held up, and the Battery received orders to move off to Tell es Sarem.

It was ascertained on arrival that the situation was somewhat relieved. Large numbers of the enemy had given themselves up, or were in the act of so doing, whilst a long column was retreating across the Jordan under cover of eight guns. The 36th Jacob's Horse, the 29th Lancers and the Middlesex Yeomanry were held up on the river banks. The Battery was accordingly brought on as fast as possible, and came into action directly, opening fire upon an enemy battery in a semi-covered position on the east bank at a range of 5,500 yards. Contact was arranged with the O.C. 29th Lancers. Almost as soon as the Battery opened fire, the Turks brought a heavy gun to bear upon it with great accuracy, and being in full view, and there being no possible cover to be obtained within effective range of the enemy, it was deemed advisable to retire the detachments from the guns. This was done under Lieut. G. E. Holberton with great calmness.

The O.C. 29th Lancers having received information from his advanced squadron that it was held up by machine-gun fire, support was called for. The detachments were at once sent back to the guns under considerable shell-fire, and fire was opened on the point called for.

This enabled the 29th Lancers to cross the ford. The 36th Jacob's Horse also called for support, and this was given, enabling the Regiment to push across the river.

At 2.15 p.m. orders were received to limber up and take a more advanced position, in order to shell the enemy column retiring to the south. Owing to the somewhat exhausted condition of the horses, after their long trot through the heavy dust, this advance was somewhat retarded. There was a large extent of boggy ground to be reconnoitred and passed, and

IN THE WOODS AT MEULEBIS. SEPT., 1918.

A TURKISH 5.9 CAPTURED AT BEISAN.

when a suitable position was reached the Column was out of range. Verbal orders were received that the Brigade was moving to Wadi Sherar, and that the Battery was to follow on.

On the night of 23rd, the Battery bivouacked with the Brigade, and on the following day information was received from an aeroplane that a force of 1,500 Turks was marching east towards Wadi Sherar, and orders were given for one Section to advance with the 29th Lancers to clear this force. It was soon found, however, that the force of the enemy was very much larger. The advanced Section was brought into action over very difficult going, on an enemy column advancing. The Rear Section was advanced as fast as possible, and came into action in the open, shelling enemy columns retiring.

The Left Section, which had been the first in action, was now again advanced to a position 500 yards south of the Right Section, and, trotting over very bad and stony country, under rifle and machine-gun fire, came into action (open sights) upon the head of the column of Turks which was now commencing to cross the Jordan. In the meantime, the Right Section had switched to the columns on the east bank. These were in even greater disorder; scattering as soon as they were clear of the gullies leading from the fords, whilst large numbers refused to face the open, and turned round and gave themselves up. Orders were given to the Left Section to advance with the 29th Lancers, and this it did, the going being extremely bad. In the meantime, the Right Section also advanced after the Left Section.

The leading Section came again into action in the open, firing open sights upon the head of a column of the enemy crossing the river. The Right Section then joined up, and a barrage was placed in front of the enemy, who were now scattering from the end of the gullies. The whole force, headed by a Divisional Commander, turned and surrendered.

The great heat had been very trying, but the men worked splendidly.

After this the Brigade moved slowly south, but owing to the exhaustion of the horses and the bad going, orders were received that the Battery would remain. Consequently, it withdrew North, where the horses were watered, the guns placed in action covering the tracks from the West, and an escort posted. Following the night's rest, orders were received, on 25th, to return to the Dorset Yeomanry at Ain Beida, and to be ready to join the Brigade on its return march to Beisan.

On 26th, the Brigade marched to Jisr Mejamie.

On 27th, the march was continued via Esh Shuni, Kharaj, and Kamm to Irbid. The first part of the way was very trying to the horses, who still suffered from their recent experiences, the roads being steep and mountainous, with " hairpin " bends, the track covered with loose stones, and the heat

I

intense.   As a result, the Battery fell far behind the Brigade, and was permitted to march in its own time.

On 28th, the Brigade marched to Er Remte, and thence to Mezerib. The 11th Cavalry Brigade, being advance brigade to the Division in its march to Sheik Miskin, reached that place at midday on 29th, where it watered in a muddy ditch, fed, and off-saddled.

Later in the day the Brigade marched to Dilli, and, arriving at 4.30 p.m., bivouacked for the night.   Good water was available, and a little grass, but there was no forage for the 30th.   At 6.30 p.m. orders were received that the Brigade would continue to march in advance of the Division to Kiswe. No water was expected after reaching Sannamein, but Kiswe proved dry, and the march was continued in great heat, over large volcanic lava stones, to Mezerib, where water was obtained in a muddy ditch, and where a halt was ordered for an hour.   At 2 p.m. the march continued, but it was found that it was not possible to reach Kiswe that night.

At 5.30 p.m. the Brigade came in touch with a Turkish rearguard, and the Battery came into action in the open upon the retreating enemy column and three guns, until darkness set in, making observation impossible.

OCTOBER, 1918.

At 9.30 a.m. on 1st October, the Brigade continued the march to Kiswe, following the 10th Brigade, in rear of the Division.

The Battery, after drawing grain, the first received for 48 hours, left Kiswe for Sbeine, where it went into bivouac for the night.

On the following day an independent march to Judeide was undertaken. On 3rd, orders were received that the horses were to be rested as far as possible.   An epidemic of malaria, probably contracted at Beisan and in the Jordan, now set in, and five other ranks were admitted to hospital.

On 5th, 17 more hospital cases occurred.   On this date Major J. K. Jeans, M.C., resumed command of the Battery, on the return of Lieutenant-Colonel O. S. Eugster.

On 6th, there were 23 further cases of malaria.   Lieutenant G. V. H. Mansell returned from the 5.9 Howitzer Detachment, of which he had been in charge since its capture at Beisan.   On this date the Brigade march to El Hame.   On succeeding days the march was continued to Khan Meizebon, and thence to Zebdani.   On 9th, Major-General Sir G. de S. Barrow personally thanked the officers of the 11th Cavalry Brigade for their work during the present operations.   Owing to the epidemic of malaria, which left the Battery 60 men under establishment, it was only possible to move by having no centre drivers on some teams, and it was no longer a fighting unit.

On 11th, the Brigade moved to El Tekkie, and thence to Zahle and

Baalbek. By 15th the Battery was not much more than a touring unit, and it became daily more difficult to give the horses the attention they required.

On 19th, orders were received to proceed with a complete Section to Aleppo, and on 20th similar orders were received in respect of the whole Battery.

On 21st, however, they were cancelled, it being decided that the Division would remain at Baalbek.

On 23rd, Lieutenant-Colonel Eugster left for the United Kingdom, and Major T. K. Jeans temporarily took over command of the 20th Brigade R.H.A.

On 24th, heavy rain fell, and the men were moved into a house near the camp.

On 25th, orders were received that the 11th Cavalry Brigade would be prepared to march at six hours' notice to Damascus. All possible arrangements were made, and it was found necessary to omit centre drivers, and for the detachments to lead three or four horses each.

On 27th, the Battery left Baalbek, halted at Tell esh Sherif, and reached Barelias. On the following day the march was continued to Khan Meizebon—a very trying march, owing to the size of the hills; and the difficulty was greatly accentuated by the conditions of reduced establishment.

At 7.30 a.m., on 29th, the Battery arrived at Damascus, and went into bivouac half a mile west of Baramie Station.

The strength of the Battery was now four officers and only 52 other ranks, and 144 horses and mules.

News had been received of the death from malaria, or the complications thereof, of 14 men of the Battery. This news cast a gloom over all their comrades.

NOVEMBER, 1918.

The strength of the Battery at the beginning of November was four officers, 52 other ranks, and 133 animals.

With such reduced personnel, it was no mean task to carry out the normal duties of watering, feeding and grooming the horses. Practically no dubbin or oil was available for the harness, and although all leather work, guns and vehicles were washed, little progress could be made in getting these in proper condition.

On 8th, Brigadier-General Gregory, C.B., inspected the horses of the Battery, and considered they had improved, but that there were a number which should be cast when an opportunity occurred.

On 11th, Lieutenant-Colonel E. H. H. Elliot, D.S.O., assumed command of 20th Brigade R.H.A., and Major T. K. Jeans, M.C., returned to the command of the Battery.

On 12th and 13th, heavy rain fell, which turned the whole bivouac area into a quagmire, and made it essential that a new bivouac should be found.

On 14th, the Battery was moved to El Mezzel, where a better standing in gravelly soil was obtained. An attempt was made to find billets in empty houses around the horse lines, but these were found to be impossible owing to vermin, and they were evacuated in favour of bivouacs. The new area was much more exposed, and the nights being very cold, the condition of the horses was not improved.

On 17th, Major T. K. Jeans, M.C., left on seven days' leave in Egypt.

On 22nd, Major Jeans proceeded to the United Kingdom on a Battery Commander's Course, commencing 15th December, from which date Major R. D. Badcock was in command.

During the month there were several inspections.

DECEMBER, 1918.

There is little to chronicle for the month of December. Normal routine and training were continued.

On 8th, 24 mule remounts were taken on strength.

On 28th, the 11th Cavalry Brigade was inspected by the G.O.C. 4th Cavalry Division.

At the conclusion of the year the Battery was still bivouacked at El Mezzel, in the vicinity of Damascus.

Appendix No. 2.

SEPTEMBER, 1918—

On 19th September, the 4th Cavalry Division, which had broken through the gap made by the infantry on the right of the main enemy positions near the sea, covered a distance of 85 miles in 37 hours and arrived at Beisan.

Here it took up a mobile defensive position across the main line of retreat of the Turkish VIIIth. Army. The latter, harassed by advancing infantry from the South, bombed and machine-gunned by our aeroplanes, was retiring in great disorder in a northerly direction towards its railways and main bases. Many confused parties of stragglers, chiefly composed of the supply and auxiliary services, had already given themselves up, having, apparently, no heart for a fight, but on the evening of 21st, soon after darkness had set in, several thousand Turks, lead by German and Austrian officers, made a strong attempt to break through that portion of our positions held by the Dorset Yeomanry.

It soon became evident to the Commanding Officer that this force of the enemy was composed of a more stubborn personnel. Artillery support was therefore called for. At 18.45 the 1/1st Hants R.H.A. opened fire from a concealed position west of Beisan.

The area on both sides of the road was swept and searched at a rapid rate of fire, with good moral effect upon the enemy, who probably had not anticipated the presence of artillery within effective range. At the same time a mounted counter-attack was being organised, and this was subsequently launched with complete success. A large number of the enemy were captured, and many more gave themselves up to the Yeomanry.

No further fighting occurred on 22nd, but our aeroplanes reported several thousands of the enemy retiring in a northerly direction, and it was therefore decided to send the 11th Cavalry Brigade (less the 1/1st Hants R.H.A.) to round up this force and prevent its escape to the East over the fords of the River Jordan.

Owing to the apparent poor state of moral of the enemy, and to a desire to save the artillery horses in the excessive heat, it was considered unnecessary for the Battery to accompany the Brigade to which it normally belonged. In the light of subsequent events, this decision was to be regretted, as it actually defeated the object in view, for the Battery arrived just too late to support the charge of the 29th Lancers, and not only had a great distance to make up, but at a fast pace, and without forage for two days.

At 06.15 the 11th Cavalry Brigade passed the Battery position, and an hour later the advance guards came in touch with a very strong body of the enemy, supported by machine-guns and two batteries of artillery. The F.O.O., who had remained with the outpost and could see the Brigade in the distance, grasped the situation, and realising that the Battery would be required at once, telephoned to the gun position a warning, thereby greatly accelerating the turn-out.

At 09.30 the Battery was ready to move off, and at 10.00 received orders from the Division to proceed as fast as possible to join the Brigade.

The track to the South was extremely rough, deeply rutted and thick in white dust; whilst the ground on either side was marshy and traversed by many streams and bogs, which rendered it impossible to quit the road.

The Battery Commander and Staff galloped to B.H.Q., where the situation was explained.

The enemy, who was retreating to the East, across the Jordan, had thrown out a strong left flank guard, supported by many machine-guns, occupying a good position, the key of which was a small hillock. This had just been very gallantly and successfully charged by a squadron of the 29th Lancers, and the main Turkish column, several thousand strong, was streaming away over the Jordan at Makhadet Abu Haj, pursued by the 36th Jacob's Horse, on the east bank, by the 29th Lancers, in the centre, and by the Middlesex Yeomanry, on the right.

Our cavalry, however was held up for the moment at the fords by machine-gun fire, and by two enemy batteries, which had been brought down on the east side from Es Salt for the purpose of providing a strong rearguard to the retiring enemy forces from the West.

In this portion of the Jordan Valley the ground slopes to the river bank in an absolutely flat, treeless plain, four miles broad, covered by low scrub, from one to two feet high.

The enemy, from his concealed positions on the east bank, had uninterrupted observation, and was able to bring fire to bear on any movement of our troops with great accurracy and speed. The Battery, smothered in dust and sweat, had trotted from Beisan, and were just coming down the slopes from the road to the west in battery column. The Battery Commander, who had just made his reconnaissance, led the Battery into action in the open 100 yards S.W. of Tell Abu Haj, and re-established observation from this hillock, on which was also situated H.Q., 29th Lancers.

With the aid of information from this regiment, fire was at once opened on the machine-guns concealed in the rough ground on the opposite bank, which were holding up the squadrons at the fords.

The enemy, who had seen the Battery manœuvring over the rough ground, and forming line for position, now turned on it a most accurate fire from his eight guns. Shells burst all around and between the guns, and three telephone wires were cut by splinters, visual signalling having to be resorted to in consequence.

The 29th Lancers reported the fords on their front clear, and it was therefore deemed advisable, owing to the continuance of the enemy's fire, to withdraw the detachments from the guns to a small ditch on the left flank.

Later, a galloper from 36th Jacob's Horse delivered a note asking for fire on two machine-guns, and describing their location by plan.

The detachments were at once led back to the guns, under increased shell-fire, and a fire was opened which enabled the 36th Jacob's Horse to advance to the South.

A large number of prisoners were taken, and the Middlesex Yeomanry succeeded in capturing the enemy batteries.

The stragglers of the enemy column were retiring to the South, along the hills on the east side of the valley, and the Battery limbered up and advanced to re-engage them.

Owing to the very marshy ground, and the long detours which were necessitated thereby, it was not possible to get within effective range.

The Battery therefore retired to the cavalry and awaited further orders, the opportunity being taken to water and feed the horses.

At 17.15 a verbal order was received from B.H.Q. to advance to Ayun-el-Beida. Darkness soon set in, and after a difficult march across country the Battery rejoined the Brigade.

Early on the morning of 24th an aeroplane report was received to the effect that 1,500 Turks were marching towards Makhadet-esh-Sherar, and orders were accordingly given for one Section of the 1/1st Hants R.H.A. to advance with the 29th Lancers to intercept them.

It was soon found that the numbers of the enemy had been greatly under-estimated, and the remaining Section was sent for. The foothills here close in on the west side almost to the river itself, and the country is traversed by deep gorges. Down one of these gorges were streaming several thousands of the enemy. The leading Section crossed the Wadi-est-Sherar, climbed up the steep bank on the south side, and came into action open sights upon this column, at a range of 3,300 yards.   Meanwhile, the enemy, caught in a confined space, and thoroughly shaken by previous fighting, streamed away up the southern slope of the gorge, in an endeavour to seek cover in the next valley.   At this moment the Rear Section, which had trotted from Ayun-el-Beida, advanced to the S.E. of the Right Section, under rifle and machine-gun fire, and came into action open sights upon this column, causing great confusion and panic.

The result was the capture of one gun and several thousands of prisoners by a squadron of the Middlesex Yeomanry.

The remainder of the enemy, having gained the cover of the southern slope, headed East, and commenced to cross the Jordan.

The Rear Section was again advanced, and the whole Battery concentrated its fire on the east bank, where the head of the column was now emerging.

On the east bank many parties of stragglers were observed, but a little further to the South there were more formed bodies, which had crossed the river unmolested.

The Battery was advanced over extremely difficult ground.   A barrage at a rapid rate of fire was put up at the head of this retiring column, and as a consequence almost the entire force turned back and gave themselves up to the Cavalry.   Of this whole enemy force, only a few stragglers and thoroughly-shaken parties had got away.

Men and horses were very exhausted from the rapid firing and from the excessive heat, and although the Brigade pushed on for three or four miles to the South, the Battery was ordered to remain where it was.

Horses were watered and fed, and as no further orders were received, the escort of one troop was posted, and the Battery bivouacked for the night.

PRISONERS TAKEN BY 29TH LANCERS. SEPT., 1918.

PRISONERS TAKEN BY THE MIDDLESEX YEOMANRY. SEPT., 1918.

Appendix No. 3.

11th CAVALRY BRIGADE.
SPECIAL ORDER.

" The General Officer Commanding desires to place on record his high appreciation of the performance of the Brigade during the recent operations, extending over the period 19th September to 1st October, 1918.

" During these twelve days the Brigade covered a distance of over 250 miles, of which the first 80 were traversed in less than 34 hours: to it, almost entirely, may be accredited the complete destruction of the 7th and 8th Turkish Armies.

" Its captures include the following:—

Prisoners of War (actually counted), of whom 233 were officers ...	...	...	...	10,615
Field Artillery Guns	...	...	...	9
Camel Guns	...	...	...	13
Machine Guns	...	...	...	87
Automatic Rifles ...	...	...	...	16
Animals ...	...	...	...	374

besides which, in its route, the enemy abandoned hundreds of thousands of rounds of ammunition, an unaccountable number of transport vehicles, and war material to the value of many thousands of pounds.

" The hardships, which naturally accompanied the operations, were borne with a cheerfulness and with an endurance beyond all praise.

" The Brigadier is glad to record that the cases of ill-discipline which have come to his notice were few, and what few did occur were confined to one unit. The Brigade may well congratulate itself on having played its part in what may justly be considered one of the greatest cavalry exploits in the annals of military history.

" The Brigadier thanks all ranks for the keenness and endurance displayed, and feels sure that should a similar call be made, the Brigade will give an equally ready answer.

" Damascus,

     " 4th October, 1918."

K

1919

JANUARY, 1919.

The month of January, 1919, found the Battery at El Mezzel. Normal routine and training continued.

One case of typhus and four cases of relapsing fever occurred, and every possible means were taken, by use of hot baths and the disinfector, to prevent the spread of these diseases.

On 16th, Lieutenant G. V. H. Mansell left the Battery, on appointment to Adjutant of the 19th Brigade R.H.A.

Lieutenant-General Sir H. G. Chauvel, K.C.B., K.C.M.G., G.O.C. Desert Mounted Corps, inspected the Battery and horses in the lines. He expressed himself very pleased with the general appearance and turn-out of the men.

During the third week a few ordnance stores arrived. None had been received for six weeks, and in consequence, both men and horses had suffered considerably, there being a shortage of nosebags, rugs, boots and breeches.

On 31st, Lieutenant Mansell was awarded the Military Cross in the New Year's Honours.

FEBRUARY.

The Battery remained at El Mezzel throughout the month of February, and there is little of note to chronicle.

On 16th, Captain Holberton, M.C., was transferred to the Berkshire R.H.A., and 2nd Lieutenant A. D. Butt was posted to the unit from the Ayrshire R.H.A.

On 5th, the History Party of C.O.'s units left for Beisan to write up the narrative of operations of September, 1918. Normal training and musketry was continued.

On 21st, there was an inspection by the G.O.C., Damascus, and on the next day the Commander-in-Chief, General Sir Edmund Allenby, made an inspection, which was followed by a march-past.

At the close of the month the strength of the Battery was three officers, 68 other ranks, 81 horses, and 21 mules. Nine other ranks had been despatched for demobilisation during the last week.

The rate of sickness was extremely low.

MARCH.

On 2nd March, Major Badcock was transferred to O.E.T.A., Jerusalem.

On 6th, there was an inspection by Sir Harry Chauvel, K.C.B., K.C.M.G.

On 19th, Captain Holberton, M.C., was posted to the unit from the Berkshire R.H.A. to take over command. Eighteen other ranks proceeded home for demobilisation, and Second-Lieutenant R. Jenkins and 16 other ranks were attached to the Battery from the 3rd Lahore Division, and 15 other ranks from 18th Brigade R.H.A.

There were also postings from the 20th B.A.C.

APRIL.

There is little to record for the month of April.

General King visited the Battery on 8th to say good-bye before proceeding home.

On 16th, there was a route march through Damascus, and there were inspections by the Brigade Commander, by the A.D.V.S. and by General Short.

Second-Lieutenant A. W. Burton joined the Battery from the 26th Brigade H.Q.

MAY.

Normal routine and training continued.

General Smith, M.G.R.A., inspected the unit in the lines on 4th May. On 9th the G.O.C., Damascus, inspected the riding drill and gun drill.

Twenty-six other ranks proceeded home, their places being filled by reinforcements from the 20th B.A.C.

JUNE.

During the month of June there is little to record.

Second-Lieutenant A. W. Burton proceeded home for demobilisation, and Second-Lieutenant W. Atkins was attached from the 20th Brigade R.H.A.

Major Baxter, from the 20th Brigade R.H.A., took over command of the Battery.

JULY.

Normal routine and training. The War Diary contains no entries of interest.

AUGUST.

On 1st August the first Race Meeting was held in Damascus.

The rate of sickness for the month was high owing to the prevalence of sandfly fever.

SEPTEMBER.

The anniversary of the victorious advance into Syria was kept as a holiday on 19th September, and there were sports.

Demobilisation continued, and certain reinforcements were received.

At the end of the month the Battery strength was four officers and 40 other ranks, to which must be added 49 Indians.

OCTOBER.

No record exists.

---◆---

Owing to the scanty material available from official War Diaries for the later period of the Battery's service abroad, the following brief summary has been contributed by Major R. D. Badcock, M.C.:—

The arrival at Baalbek marked the end of operations as far as the 4th Cavalry Division was concerned. It had suffered heavy casualties on the long and arduous march: comparatively few in action, many from malaria and Spanish influenza, and during the first few days' halt at Baalbek so many more casualties occurred from sickness that eventually it ceased to be mobile as a fighting force. And so, although at first it was intended that the whole Division should march to Aleppo in support of the 5th Cavalry Division, and afterwards that a modified Division—i.e., a squadron per regiment and a section per battery—should undertake the march, eventually the Divisional Commander had to report that his Division was unfit for further active operations until some of his casualties had been made good, and the Australian Mounted Division was ordered to go forward instead. This meant that one Brigade of the 4th Cavalry Division had to move back to Damascus for duty on lines of communication. In accordance with this order, on October 22nd the 11th Cavalry Brigade moved back. It was a very different body of men to the Brigade that started out on operations a month earlier. The Indian regiments had suffered least, they were, possibly, at half strength; the Middlesex Yeomanry consisted of two officers and a troop; the M.G. Squadron, two officers and a Section; the Hants Battery, four officers, 60 men and full complement

DAMASCUS : THE FORTRESS AND TOWN.

of guns and wagons. As can readily be seen, it was a trying march for the Battery, the horses were thoroughly tired out, there were no gunners —every one was a driver or horse-holder—and even at that there were no centre drivers. However, the journey (some 70 miles) was made in the usual three stages. Halting the first night at Shtora and the second at Khan Meizebun, Damascus was reached on the third day. That may be considered the last exploit of the Battery. The Armistice with Turkey was signed on November 1st, and the Battery remained at Damascus as part of the army of occupation until the cadre was sent home in October, 1919.

The year spent in Damascus provides a poor story, of which the keynote is monotony, and no one who spent an appreciable time there can look back on it with any great pleasure. It is a thoroughly pleasant place in which to spend a few days.

The town itself is full of interest to the sightseer, the big mosque and the bazaars cannot fail to excite admiration, and not less wonderful are the business methods of the merchant, who is quite depressed if his goods are bought at his first-named figure, and much prefers the intending purchaser to suggest a quarter of the sum, this giving a nice margin over which to argue. No one can view the wonderful blaze of the desert sunrise, with mosque and minaret of the big city standing out all hazy in front of it, or the wonderful deep green of the orchards, which cover many acres east and south of the city, without one added thrill. But all this applies to the sightseer: the ordinary mortal who is stationed long in the district looks for some more exciting recreation than sight-seeing, and all men hate sunrise from force of habit. Recreation ground was always a difficulty, owing to the rocky nature of the surrounding country—football grounds, however well cleared, were dangerous, and casualties were frequent. In November the rains set in, and rain and wind were constant companions till the end of February, and be it known, the wind that blew from the snow of Hermon was neither good for man nor beast. Supplies were again a difficulty during the winter months. Constant wash-outs and bridge troubles on the Haifa-Damascus line did not allow the supply officer much scope, and even Q.-M.-S. Meaney could get little more than the bare ration. In matter of canteen stores there was nothing doing till February, and what beer succeeded in getting through the stiff barrage at the base was trapped by the divisions in Ludd area, and what leaked through their rapacious grasp was a mere trickle. However, the Battery, on arrival at Damascus, was at first camped in an orchard on the Mezze-Damascus road—the men in bivouacs and the officers in a clean house near by shared with Middlesex Yeomanry and M.G.C. officers—but this was not for long, as the rains came and washed horses and men out of the orchard, and a reinforcement of Middlesex officers had much the same effect on the officers. A move was therefore made to an open space in Mezzel village. The Right Section horse lines were first put up in a walled compound, protected to some extent from winds; the Left Section just outside. The place had the advantage of being well drained and close to water. The Right Section tried sleeping in the house in their compound for one night, and suffered a severe defeat—that peculiarly loathsome insect, the boon companion of the Turk, came out of the walls in thousands and tens of thousands and drove the sleepers out of the house on to the terrace outside, but even there they were not safe, as the victors, flushed with success and regardless of cold, swarmed out of doors and windows and chased the now demoralised Section further afield. Soon after this tents were issued, and henceforth houses were left severely alone. Soon after the move Major Jeans was ordered to U.K. for a gunnery course, and Captain Badcock took command of the Battery.

Although reinforcements had joined the Battery and several old gunners and drivers who went sick in the Jordan Valley returned, yet there was a a considerable shortage in personnel, and a good deal of the work was done by Turkish prisoners. These men were in a miserable state when captured, but were willing to work as far as their strength allowed; but in a very few weeks, on the more generous ration allowed by the British, they became as fat as pigs and fully as lazy. The ordinary daily routine was not inspiring, and is not worthy of recording, but Christmas Day certainly deserves notice, both because of the great pains taken by certain members of the Battery in making the preparations, and because of the success that attended their efforts. A trip to Beirut by Lieutenant Perry produced beer and canteen stores, many journeys to Damascus by Lieutenant Carr produced chicken and ingredients for plum puddings, and the energy of the Quartermaster and cooks supplied the rest, which took the form of a most excellent Christmas dinner. Afterwards a football match was played against a battery of the 3rd Division, and though some of the team had dined very well, if not too wisely—at any rate, obviously much better than their opponents—when set upon their legs, they played like men, and were only beaten by the odd goal.

A concert got up by the Middlesex Yeomanry soon after Christmas is worthy of mention, as it was the last occasion on which the famous Battery Quartette performed—as usual, theirs were the best items on a very excellent programme.

In the Divisional football competition the Battery produced a good team, and was unlucky not to go far in the competition. In the preliminary rounds, which were decided by Brigades, the Battery was drawn against

"TOSS UP" AT THE FINAL OF THE YEOMANRY CUP.
I/IST HANTS R.H.A. *v.* BERKS R.H.A.   MARCH, 1918.

the 21st Machine Gun Squadron, and beat them after a hard game by 5 to 1, but had to play the Middlesex Yeomanry the next day, when several members of the team were crocked by falls on the stoney ground, and lost by 1 goal to nothing.

In January demobilisation began, and from then onwards men began to drift away to the U.K., at first slowly, but afterwards quickly. This was a most unsettling time for every one, and the system pursued by the Authorities caused a good deal of heart-burning; but men kept their tempers well and their private opinions to themselves, so no regrettable incidents occurred, as was the case in some units. In February camp was moved for the last time; as a few cases of typhus fever broke out among the troops, the medical authorities decided that Mezzel village area was not healthy for troops to live in, and moved the Brigade out to the 3rd Infantry Divisional area, just outside the village, only leaving the hospital in the village itself.

In the middle of March demobilisation stopped for a time, owing to the outbreak of riots in Egypt. Intensive training was carried on once more, and all ranks buckled too like true sportsmen, in spite of obvious disappointment at the turn of affairs. And when the troops of Damascus area marched through the city to impress the inhabitants, the Battery was second to none in turn-out. However, before the end of May demobilisation opened up again, and by the beginning of June all ranks of the old Battery, except a few who had volunteered for army of occupation, had left for home.

———◆———

ROLL OF FALLEN.

The following roll of casualties for the Battery is taken from the official publication—" Soldiers Died in the Great War, 1914-1919. Part 2. Section 6 (Royal Horse and Royal Field Artillery, Territorial Force, including Honourable Artillery Company Batteries)."

EXPLANATION OF ABBREVIATIONS.

B.   ...   ...   Born   D. of W. ...   ... Died of Wounds
E.   ...   ...   Enlisted   K. in A. ...   .. Killed in Action
D.   ...   ...   Died

When the place of enlistment is followed by the name of another place in brackets, the latter represents the deceased soldier's place of residence.

WILLIS-FLEMING, RICHARD THOMAS CYRIL—Lieutenant; K. in A., August 4th, 1916.

BANGER, ALFRED WILLIAM—B. Plaistow; E. Southampton; 618111, Trptr.;
  D. Egypt., October 17, 1918.
BLACKLEDGE, HARRY—B. N.S.W., Australia; E. Sheffield; 608220, A/Bdr.;
  D. Palestine, October 14th, 1918.
CHAFER, JOHN—B. Rotherham; E. Wentworth, Yorks; 608120, Dvr.;
  D. Egypt, October 15th, 1918.
COURTNEY, ALBERT EDWARD—B. Botley, Southampton; E. Southampton;
  618099, Dvr.; D. Palestine, October 12th, 1918.
FLETCHER, CHARLES HENRY—B. Southampton; E. Southampton; 618100,
  Bdr.; D. Egypt, October 13th, 1918.
FREEBORN, CHARLES JAMES—B. Basingstoke; E. Southampton; 618041,
  Cpl.; D. Palestine, October 14th, 1918.
MEANEY, NORMAN WESTON—B. Southampton; E. Southampton; 618062,
  Dvr.; D. Palestine, October 20th, 1918.
RUDGE, ARTHUR—B. Bournemouth; E. Southampton; 618158, Dvr.;
  D. Egypt, October 12th, 1918.
STUBBINS, RICHARD—B. Walthamstow, Essex; E. Leonard Street, E.C.;
  671050, Dvr.; D. Palestine, October 6th, 1918.
WARD, FREDERICK—E. Rotherham (Rotherham); 608085, Gnr.; D. Egypt,
  October 12th, 1918.
WARREN, JOHN EDWARD—B. Southampton; E. Southampton; 618292,
  Gnr.; D. Egypt, October 16th, 1918.

AWARDS.

Major T. K. Jeans ... M.C.	Lieut. G. V. H. Mansell... M.C.	
Capt. R. D. Badcock ... M.C.	Lieut. R. Bazell ... M.C.	
Lieut. T. E. Holberton M.C. and Bar		

618047 Sergeant Brewster, R. ... ... D.C.M. and M. in D.
618008 B.Q.M.S. Meaney, E. W. ... ... D.C.M. and M. in D.
618001 Sergt. (A./B.S.M.) Hitchcock, W. G. D.C.M. and M. in D.
608061 Sergeant Schofield, A. ... ... D.C.M.
618013 Bombr.-Sig. Manning, R. F. ... M.M.
618059 Gunner-Sig. Wiltshire, F. G. ... M.M.
618197 Gunner Caplen, E. J. ... ... M.M.
618089 Pd. L/Bombr. Neville, F. W. ... M. in D. Subsequently
                                          became Second-Lieut.
                                          R.F.A. (S.R.).
608025 Sergeant Tuxford, S. ... ... M.M.

www.ingramcontent.com/pod-product-compliance
Lightning Source LLC
Chambersburg PA
CBHW050918150426
42812CB00050B/1801